General editor: Graham Handley MA Ph.D.

Brodie's Notes on

The Metaphysical Poets

Graham Handley MA Ph.D.
Formerly Principal Lecturer in English and Head of English Department,
College of All Saints, Tottenham

MACMILLAN

First published by Pan Books Ltd 1981
This edition published 1991

Published by
MACMILLAN PRESS LTD
Houndmills, Basingstoke, Hampshire RG21 6XS
and London
Companies and representatives
throughout the world

ISBN 0–333–58115–6

This book is printed on paper suitable for recycling and made from fully managed and sustained forest sources.

10   9   8   7   6   5   4   3
03   02   01   00   99   98   97   96

Printed in Great Britain by
Mackays of Chatham PLC
Chatham, Kent

Contents

Preface by the general editor   5

An introduction to metaphysical poetry   7

Notes on individual poets and poems,
with revision questions
Thomas Carew   9
Richard Crashaw   18
John Donne   28
George Herbert   61
Richard Lovelace   78
Andrew Marvell   83
John Wilmot, Earl of Rochester   98
Sir John Suckling   103
Henry Vaughan   107

General questions   120

Page references in the Notes are to the Penguin edition
of *The Metaphysical Poets* (ed. Helen Gardner,
1957 revised 1972), but the poets and poems are
discussed in alphabetical order, so that the Notes may
be used with any edition of the poems.

Preface

The intention throughout this study aid is to stimulate and guide, to encourage your involvement in the book, and to develop informed responses and a sure understanding of the main details.

Brodie's Notes provide a clear outline of the play or novel's plot, followed by act, scene, or chapter summaries and/or commentaries. These are designed to emphasize the most important literary and factual details. Poems, stories or non-fiction texts combine brief summary with critical commentary on individual aspects or common features of the genre being examined. Textual notes define what is difficult or obscure and emphasize literary qualities. Revision questions are set at appropriate points to test your ability to appreciate the prescribed book and to write accurately and relevantly about it.

In addition, each of these Notes includes a critical appreciation of the author's art. This covers such major elements as characterization, style, structure, setting and themes. Poems are examined technically – rhyme, rhythm, for instance. In fact, any important aspect of the prescribed work will be evaluated. The aim is to send you back to the text you are studying.

Each study aid concludes with a series of general questions which require a detailed knowledge of the book: some of these questions may invite comparison with other books, some will be suitable for coursework exercises, and some could be adapted to work you are doing on another book or books. Each study aid has been adapted to meet the needs of the current examination requirements. They provide a basic, individual and imaginative response to the work being studied, and it is hoped that they will stimulate you to acquire disciplined reading habits and critical fluency.

Graham Handley 1991

An introduction to metaphysical poetry

Most anthologies of poetry contain an introduction to individual poets and the time at which they wrote, together with some consideration of the literary styles and the tradition they inherited. The metaphysical poets of the seventeenth century, led by John Donne, were reacting against the courtly love poetry of the Elizabethans, but it would be wrong to think of the metaphysical poets as a school or a group or as having any common policy. The sonnet and the lyric, the couplet and the more formally structured verses were part of the Elizabethan stylistic concern, but they were adapted by Donne and infused with a wider implication and a wider range of imagery too. The dictionary definition of the metaphysicals is as good a starting point as any: they 'combined intense feeling with ingenious thought and often used elaborate imagery and conceits'. This is true, and is what led Dr Johnson to comment on their use of 'heterogeneous ideas yoked by violence together'. Nevertheless they gave to English poetry, in the platitude of our times, a new dimension. 'Sea-discoverers to new worlds had gone', and Donne was quick to use this kind of contemporary event to give to his own poetry a width of application that went far beyond the Elizabethan court. For any student of the metaphysicals a good beginning is to read Carew's *Elegie on the death of Dr John Donne*, for there he will find the poet's assessment of what the great master achieved. But perhaps here we should indicate in outline the main facets of metaphysical verse.

1 The use of traditional forms, i.e. like the sonnet, but infused with an individuality, an occasional abruptness (often in the opening lines), frequently a colloquial tone. A breaking with the smooth flow where appropriate, with rhetorical or conversational or elevated turns, sometimes with imagery drawn from the period or from science, scholasticism, the Bible or devotional writings.

2 The use of wit – elaborate figurative treatments of a particular subject – and employing epigram, paradox, contraries, or personified abstractions. The full range cannot be covered here, but

a study of individual poems will show how the method develops in the different poets.

3 The use of the sensual and the intellectual where appropriate – sometimes the linking of the spiritual and the intellectual.

4 The expression of personal feeling with directness and intensity on the one hand, or in the form of an intellectual, perhaps learned, dialogue on the other.

5 The use of the lyric, not as a conventional exercise but as an emotional or devotional expression.

6 The inclusion not merely of learned allusions in the poems, but of new knowledge as well – in mathematics, science, geography, biology.

7 The use of satire and irony, sometimes involving the esoteric, since there is a private language and sometimes a private joke in metaphysical poetry.

8 The use of a microcosmic emphasis, a tendency to interpret life in a particular way.

9 The use of the individual voice as against that of poetic convention.

10 The idea of living for the present, sometimes combined with the contemplation of death.

11 A considerable interest in the soul, in both the religious and philosophical areas.

Thomas Carew
(1594/5–1640)

The poet and his work

Carew's father was of Cornish landed gentry descent, and his mother the daughter and granddaughter of Lord Mayors of London. The Carews lived at West Wickham in Kent and moved to Chancery Lane in London in 1603. Little is known of Thomas's early career, save that in 1608 he went up to Merton College, Oxford. He took his degree in 1611, and was awarded a Cambridge BA in 1612. His intention was to practise law, and he entered the Middle Temple in 1612. He stayed in Italy in 1613–14, arriving back in London in 1615. Next Carew went on an embassy to the Netherlands, but was sent home in disgrace, apparently for libelling his employers, Sir Dudley and Lady Carleton. He now had to find another patron, and spent some time in loose living and debauchery, thoroughly disliked by his ageing father, who died in 1618. In the following year Carew went on an embassy to Paris with Lord Herbert of Cherbury, and indeed he may well have spent the next few years in France. His first poems appeared in 1622; certainly the most important and audacious of his poems 'in the amorous Way' was 'The Rapture', a frankly sensual narrative of sexual experience, couched in the imagery but going beyond the conventions of the day:

Yet my tall pine shall in the Cyprian strait,
Ride safe at anchor, and unlade her freight.

In 1630 Carew obtained a position at Court, became friends with his fellow poet Aurelian Townsend, and wrote a noble elegy (included in the selection here) on the death of Donne. His masque *Coelum Britannicum* was performed in February 1634. By 1638 he had become very friendly with Suckling, who satirized him for the slowness of his inspiration. From 1638 onwards Carew appeared to those who knew him to be more repentant and religious than before. In later life his health deteriorated – he had probably contracted syphilis in the 1618–19 period – and he died in March 1640. He left behind one or two fine lyrics, and the noble elegy on Donne, as well as a variety of light verse in the convention of the time, and an impressive masque. 'The Rapture' is one of the finest sexual poems in the language, for while it employs much traditional language it also transcends that language by the power of its sensual appeal and the deployment of its wit. Carew is a minor poet, but a minor poet of some distinction, as the following extracts will show.

Poem summaries, textual notes and revision questions
Boldenesse in love

A sonnet-type composition with sixteen lines instead of fourteen. The commonplace poetic image of the marigold refusing to open until the sun shines is the theme of the first few lines, with the sun arriving and opening the flower – just as the lover will arrive at his destiny by constant professions of love, to be finally admitted by Celia.

amorous Because it sleeps with the sun.
Planet of the day The sun.
virgin leaves Obviously preparing for the movement of the subject to Celia.
fond Attentive, doting.
discover Reveal.

An Elegie upon the death of the Deane of *Pauls,* Dr *John Donne*

First printed in 1633 with a number of other elegies upon the author, which makes the invocation of the first few lines rather superfluous. After indicating the inadequacies of plain Church and religious conformity, the poet goes on to praise, in rhetorical but finely controlled language, the particular qualities of Donne: the mixture of intellect and passion in his work, his insight into the rich heart of things; what a later poet, Christopher Smart, was to refer to as:

The multitudinous abyss,
Where Secrecy remains in bliss,
And wisdom hides her skill.

Carew examines the state of English poetry before Donne came to purge it and plant 'fresh invention'; these inventions replaced the imitative and derivative nature of poetic convention at the time and Donne is fit to be ranked with the very best poets. By this Carew means the great names of classical time, and praises Donne for the quality of his imagination and the masculinity of his language. He foresees, though, a reaction against Donne and his practices by the minor poets of the time, and then asks forgiveness for daring to interrupt his funeral with these lines, for he knows that Donne will react violently to this 'Crowne of Bayes' which is being put upon him. He ends with the fine Epigraph which so accurately mirrors Donne's achievement, his independence, the curious combination within him – at least in its intensity – of lover and priest, which characterized his writing at the beginning and the end.

This is a noble poem, the couplets sonorous with sadness and with the rhythms of a funeral march. The language and the images and the range of reference indicate Carew's quality when he is writing at his best. The structure of the poem shows, too, his acute awareness of form.

widdowed By the death of Donne.
dowe-bak't 'Dough-baked'; this clearly indicates the heavy and uninspired Church commentary on the death of the Dean of St Paul's.
uncisor'd With uncut hair (in token of mourning).
Dry as the sand that measures it A fine way of indicating the dullness and lack of inspiration in tributes to Donne from the Churchmen.
Committed holy Rapes upon our Will Surely an image that Donne would have appreciated.
the melting heart distill i.e. conveyed your warmth and humanity too.
As sense might judge Notice the antithetical balance of this line and the fact that it shows two of Donne's salient features – his intellect and his imagination.
Delphique quire i.e. at Delphi, where the oracle was.
Promethean breath Prometheus 'breathed' fire; he stole it from heaven and was punished by Zeus. The implication is that Donne breathed fire into English poetry.
The Muses garden Again imagery which would have been greatly appreciated by Donne, as we have seen in 'To Mr *Rowland Woodward*', where Donne refers to 'love-song weeds, and Satyrique thorns'.
penurious Poverty stricken (in terms of poetry).
Mimique i.e. imitation.
Anacreons ... Pindars Anacreon was a Greek lyric poet, born about 570 BC, Pindar the Greek lyric poet born about 522 BC.
not their owne i.e. they were 'servile' imitators.
open'd Us a Mine Part of the tribute here lies in the fact that Donne

himself used this kind of image, particularly in his love poems.

masculine expression A direct reference to Donne's uncompromising ruggedness and breaking with convention ('I wonder by my troth').

Orpheus The legendary pre-Homeric poet who went to retrieve his wife Eurydice from the underworld but, having been warned not to do so, looked back at her, and so lost her for ever.

Exchequer i.e. you were the central paying-out place – they all drew credit from you (they copied you).

blinde fate of language The implication is that Donne's appeal can only suffer through changes in taste, which Carew regards as superficial and lacking in Donne's substance.

tough-thick-rib'd hoopes A metaphor: Donne's imagination and strength of utterance had burst the bonds of containment of the literary corset or strait-jacket of 'soft melting Phrases'.

soft melting Phrases i.e. weak sentimental poetry.

To touch their Harvest Almost a continuation of the earlier growth images of nature which are consonant with the cultivation undertaken by Donne; 'gleaned' and 'reape' are also a deliberate continuation of this.

Libertines Loose livers, here those without discipline.

Metamorphoses A series of mythological tales by Ovid (43BC–AD18), really a collection of the principal myths of Greece and Rome.

Turne ballad rime i.e. is cheapened.

untun'd Discordant, but perhaps suitable here to the mood and to what Donne achieved.

Idolls . . . new apostasie The idea is that the pagan conventions will be re-invoked by these poets who haven't the wit or imagination to take heed of what Donne has achieved. The result will be false worship again.

in these panting numbers i.e. feeble verses – and note the death image that accompanies this, and is consonant with the subject of the poem: the death of Donne and the death of a particular body of poetry.

the swiftly turning wheele i.e. which we have set in motion, again the kind of image that Donne might have used (compare it with the circles in water of 'Love's Growth').

crowne of Bayes The bay tree, a shrub of the Laurel family was used by the ancient Romans to crown victorious generals.

draw the envy to engrosse Perhaps 'thee' is meant – I will not create jealousy (by drawing up a list of your perfections).

Theme enough to tyre all Art i.e. you are so complete and outstanding that Art would be exhausted in trying to describe you.

incise Chisel, write.

The universall Monarchy of wit i.e. the kingdom of true poetic utterance.

Flamens Particular priests.

Maria Wentworth

She was second daughter of Thomas Wentworth, Earl of Cleveland and she died in 1632 at the age of eighteen. Carew's verses, with some differences, are inscribed on Maria's tomb, where she is shown with a sewing-basket. She is thought to have died after pricking her finger. The tone is typical, and what was expected. There are seven verses, three lines in each in the form of a triplet. Maria is seen as an angel, as one spreading love, loyal and dutiful to her parents, kind to everybody; though a virgin she was married to all that was good, an example to the world, of goodness and what we must all come to.

temper'd Formed (body).
guest The soul, the individual (the real inner Maria).
a Cherubin i.e. innocent or sweet, angelic.
shind Shone.
cleare Loyal, reliable.
Poligamie i.e. married to more than one (here to every virtue).

Mediocritie in love rejected

A typical Carew song, and the theme is typical too of many love lyrics, from Petrarch onwards. The idea is that love or hate, whichever extreme, is preferable to 'the temperate zone'. In fact the form is a kind of sonnet reversed, with six lines (alternate lines rhyming, followed by a couplet) and then eight lines (alternate lines rhyming followed by two couplets). The final line is a straight repetition of the first.

Torrid i.e. passion.
frozen i.e. coldness.
estate i.e. state of being.
Like *Danae* in that golden showre Jove ravished Danae by descending on her as a shower of gold.
Vulture-hopes i.e. his predatory desires, his sexual will.

Perswasions to enjoy

As with 'Mediocritie in love rejected', a kind of reverse sonnet, six then eight lines, but this time all in lilting couplets. The theme is the theme of 'The Rapture': let us love while we can

quick spirits i.e. indicative of life and desire.
Must fly Change with time.
reape ... fruit Common imagery of the period.
golden fleece Her hair.
bright Suns Her eyes.
Thus, either *Time*. . . i.e. either Time will change you, or we must make the most of time now.

Song

This fine lyric is in five verses in which the couplet is given a rare musical quality. The alliterative effects rise and fall like the melody, and the conceit is the comparison of the poet's love with all that is beautiful in nature, with the mistress taking from nature the beauties as they fade, for in her they remain at their peak. In the very essence of the lady is the rose, in the very essence of light is her hair, the nightingale's song is saved in her throat, the essence of the comets or shooting stars is in her sight, while the Phoenix (that symbol of the rekindling of life and thus the permanence of love), is within her. The quality of expression is exquisite throughout; the control and the limpid texture of the verse give us this kind of courtly lyric at its very best. There is a slight twist in the last verse.

Jove Jupiter, King of the Roman Gods.
These flowers as in their causes i.e. distilled from their finest essence.
the golden Atomes of the day The essence of light.
downewards fall Shooting stars or comets.
as in their sphere The heavens, the night sky.
Phoenix The fabulous bird, supposedly unique, which consumes itself by fire on its own funeral pyre, and then arises from the ashes.

To a Lady that desired I would love her

Seven verses of five lines each, with alternate lines rhyming but a climaxing couplet to each verse. The first is in the form of a rhetorical question asking the lady if she will torment him, now that she has given him leave to approach her; the second urges her to create love (anyone can destroy it); the third, for them to love each other and not for effect; the fourth urges her to make joy rather than grief; the fifth attacks the poetic conventions of familiar images used to convey hurt or suffering. The last two verses indicate the poet's own self-mocking tendency as he sees himself praising his mistress in just the terms that all poets use.

pettie Cheap, common.
Spight In spite of.
Dispence Give out.
you may create i.e. you may inspire a love – or written expressions of that love.
designe The motive of.
puling Whimpering (note the derogatory nature of the term here).
blubbr'd eyne i.e. their weeping eyes (because they have been rejected).
layes Poetic utterances.
chearfull numbers Happy poems.
nets Traps (because of her attractions).
Suborning Perjuring, wronging.
Suns . . . Crystall Conventional, superficial, poetic figures: the poet is mocking himself.
your mine of Pleasure i.e. grants him the pleasure of making love to her, yields up her virginity. This is typical of Carew, who can pass from the conventional to the sensual with rare ease.

To *Ben. Jonson* Upon occasion of his Ode of defiance annext to his Play of the new Inne

This play by one of Shakespeare's great contemporaries was booed from the stage in 1629. It was published two years after its dramatic failure, and Jonson attacked the taste of the age in terms calculated to upset that age completely. Thus he was attacked and defended, and this is one of the defences of the play and his principles. Carew notes the attack, then traces Jonson's own dramatic concerns. Other dramatists are compared to geese (Jonson's plays are swans), but he implies that Jonson has no need – so great is he – to comment on the age in which he writes. Let all their censure be thrown at him, and let them too feast on the praise of the time, which is superficial. Jonson is unquestionably the greatest dramatist of the time.

sotted Inferior, self-important.
the *Alchymist* *The Alchemist*, one of Jonson's most celebrated 'humours' comedies.
a red/ And blushing evening Literally, a red sunset, but the implication is that Jonson has changed direction somewhat – probably his writing is becoming more realistic and hence offends some.

thy Eaglets i.e. children (here, plays).

Trickt up in Dressed up in, costumed.

thy births deform'd? i.e. your plays ill-shaped or constructed.

Citie-custome ... *Gavell-kind* After death, a tenant's land was shared equally between his children in this form of land tenure.

thy ytch of praise i.e. itch (need) to be commended or praised (here seen as a weakness in Jonson, or at least a criticism of him).

drouth Drought, shortage.

Rowte Common people, public.

a *Goodwin* frame A reference to the treacherous Goodwin sands off Ramsgate.

thy watchfull Lampe As a light while he writes.

Tapers thriftie waste Such use of a light.

sleeks i.e. makes smooth (a reference to the style of the poems).

A knottie writer, bring the bootie home i.e. if you triumph over a difficult writer, turn it to advantage.

from conquered Authors i.e. those you have studied – (use or display what you have found).

after dayes The future.

Th'abortive off-spring i.e. the poor poems or plays.

Virge i.e. your own level, on your own terms (strictly an area under the jurisdiction of the Lord High Steward, but here Jonson's own superior domain).

The wiser world Those who are wise think you greater than anyone else.

To my inconstant Mistris

Another song, this time with the poet asserting that his faith will safeguard him against the vagaries of his mistress. She will curse herself for having lost him, and he compares the joys of his own faith in the love-terms he might once have used of her. The religious associations run throughout, and reinforce the strength of this song, which has five lines in each verse, with alternate rhymes and a couplet at the end of each.

excommunicate A term used to indicate rejection from the faith, with Love here replacing the Religion we should expect.

A fayrer hand ... glory crown'd i.e. of God (or is he referring to her human successor?).

Damn'd for ... Apostasie Condemned for falseness (strictly, 'abandonment or renunciation of one's religious faith', *OED*).

To my worthy friend Master *George Sands*

Again the measure is the rhyming couplet. These are commendatory lines, the poet not presuming to 'polute' things divine, but standing, as the ancients did, listening to the liturgies of the Church. At the same time her feels as a fellow-poet somehow in touch with the writer, and that his own verse may in consequence gain a more religious note. He may change from a sensual mode to a reverential one [thus following John Donne], and the poem ends on a strong penitential note.

Quire Variant spelling of 'choir', with a religious tone here.
unwasht Impure, not cleansed spiritually.
layes Hymns, songs; here, psalms.
a lay-place Outside the chosen ones, but proper and in due order.
Vestments Garments, robes (of a church dignitary).
the Arke Emphasizing the idea of the psalms being a Covenant with God.
the Sun Perhaps a pun on 'son' of God, i.e. Christ.
penitentiall dew Weeping in repentance.
brine . . . sensuall love Note the parallel with Donne, who moved from sensuality to religious identification and responsibility.
fire may be quencht/With fire i.e. sexual passion quenched by religious passion.
cloy'd i.e. had so much that it cannot be appreciated.
moulds of clay Human bodies.
indite Write.
verdant Bay i.e. the 'laurels' of the poet. (See note on 'crowne of Bayes', p.12)
Golgotha The place of skulls, Calvary.
Thorne i.e. symbolic of suffering, as with Christ's crown of thorns.

Revision questions on Thomas Carew

1 Write a critical appreciation of any *two* of Carew's Songs.

2 What are the main arguments put forward in praise of either Donne or Ben Jonson in Carew's poems about them? You should refer closely to the text in your answer.

3 In what ways is Carew more than just a court poet? You may refer to two or three poems in your answer.

4 What have you found in Carew's poems that fits the definition of 'metaphysical'? Again, you should refer closely to the poems concerned and quote in your answer.

Richard Crashaw
(1612–1649)

The poet and his work

Crashaw's birth date is given variously as 1612 and 1613; he was
the son of a Puritan preacher of some talent and impeccable
piety, and was educated at Charterhouse and Pembroke College,
Cambridge. In 1634 he took his BA, and in the following year
was awarded a Fellowship at Peterhouse. At this period, five
years before the Puritan Revolution, Peterhouse was the main
centre of support for the High Church principles of Archbishop
Laud which aroused such opposition in the country at large.
Crashaw seems to have been closely connected with the Church
at this period, being a frequent visitor to the religious com-
munity at Little Gidding which had been founded by Nicholas
Ferrar (and which was to provide the source for a great poet of
the twentieth century, in his *Four Quartets* – T. S. Eliot).

Crashaw himself described the kind of life there in his 'Description of a Religious House'. He was personally ascetic, and
most of his actions and writings subserved spiritual ends. In
1643 Peterhouse was inspected by a Parliamentary Commission,
and Crashaw – who already had Roman Catholic leanings and
refused to take the Protestant Covenant – lost his Peterhouse
fellowship; these leanings also prevented him from receiving
Anglican orders. Crashaw then left Cambridge for the Continent, where he stayed only a short time before returning to
England and staying at Oxford; he later travelled to Paris. He
was converted to Roman Catholicism, and went to Rome; and
from there to Loreto, the shrine of the Virgin, where he died.
The edition of his poems entitled *Carmen Deo Nostro* was published in 1652, after his death.

Poem summaries, textual notes and revision questions
And he answered them nothing

This six-line exercise in rhyming couplets is a play on the word
Nothing, out of which God created the Universe. It is a brief
comment on the state of the contemporary life, which is as

nothing. This is the language of rhetoric, playing on the idea of the creation and God's silence (i.e. saying nothing) when man was saved by Christ.

Charitas Nimia: or the Deare Bargain

Adapted from Psalms, viii,4: 'What is man, that thou are mindful of him?' The idea initially is that God perhaps considers man too much but the idea quickly transfers itself to Love, who is too kind. Heaven would exist without man, so let man weep over his own wounds. Crashaw continued in this strain: God would still be adored, the Sun still continue in his race; why waste any time on 'some foolish flye'. The imagery is switched a little, so that the Lamb should not be made to bleed for the sin of the wolf. But in a verse that returns to the octosyllabic couplets at the end, the poet asks God always to remind him of how much he – God – has paid for man. Couplets alternate with alternate-line rhyming in a poem that is an elaborate conceit on the theme of rejection, but with an overtone at the end making clear the sacrifice of God for man and man's recognition of it. The sting, or here the paradox, is in the tail.

over-bought Paid too much for.
sorry merchandise Feeble bargaining.
Seraphims The fiery-winged angels.
ever-wakeful sonnes Angels.
froward dust Mankind.
peevish clay Wayward man.
Eternitie Beyond time.
wanton Irresponsible.
call'd for a floud A flood of tears.
Death ... Love Again the balancing finality of this; notice how all the
 arguments are simply defeated by this statement.

An Hymne of the Nativity, sung as by the Shepheards

Written in a choric form and full of repetitions as one would expect in a hymn of celebration; most marked is the use of contrarieties, which is the employment of seeming contradictions for effect. The first chorus invoked the sun in praise, for he has not yet seen the new King, i.e. Christ. Tityrus is asked to tell the sun the news. He is aided and abetted by Thyrsis, and both of them bless the arrival of the Infant. They ponder on the poverty of the manger and the coldness of the snow. The seraphim (here 'Seraphins') also greet the arrival of the child. Gradually this works up to a full chorus in which the contrarieties are fully uttered, with the emphasis on the humble attendants on the King, i.e. the shepherds. The final lines indicate the sacrifice of the shepherds for the new King; the sacrifice is their old way of life. Repetition, paradox or contrariety, the usual ransacking of a wealth of imagery, some connected with the theme, some not, these are the common constituents of this poem and many others by Crashaw.

Loves noone ... Natures night The first of the contrarieties – the height of Love though born at night.
well-stoln i.e. goodness stolen into our world.
ought Anything.
TITYRUS ... THYRSIS Traditional shepherds' names, from the Greek.
darknesse ... day Another deliberate contrast for effect.
to wage his wars i.e. to be violent (the North wind).
Contend Get together (to produce).
The Phoenix See note p.14.
embraves i.e. makes braver, and makes the morning better too.
Seraphins See note p.19.
Eternitie shut in a span i.e. immortality, timelessness, here in the form of the babe.
Sister-Seas i.e. the breasts of the Virgin Mary.
Mother-Diamonds ... young Eagles eyes i.e. the eyes of the Virgin and the eyes of Jesus.
gay flyes/Guilded i.e. courtiers.
Slippery soules i.e. because dependent on the favour of the King.
Well read ... simplicity i.e. dutiful in their humility.
Maia's The eldest of the seven Pleiades, mother of Hermes by Zeus.
Lamb Christ.
Our selves become i.e. we become devoted to you (Christ).

Hymn to Sainte Teresa

This, one of Crashaw's better poems, is written in the octosyllabic couplet. St Teresa is a figure worthy of devotion, and we note that she was the foundress of an order of Carmelites. She tried to martyr herself as a child by attempting to convert the Moors; she was made a saint in 1622, some forty years after her death. The first invocation is to the established saints, those who courted death by their defence of the Lord. The poet reverts to the childhood of St Teresa, emphasizing, above all, the word 'Love' as emblematic of her, even in her weakness as a child. Love wants above all to fulfil itself, and consequently the urge to martyrdom is strong, though Teresa has to travel for it. She will convert the Moors, but in fact she must be called back 'T' embrace a milder Martyrdome'. She must be reserved for a more mystical and noble death, and the vision which she saw of the seraphim plunging a dart into her heart is now invoked. She will feel all the joys of heaven, for the angels will greet her. All her good works on earth shall be rewarded, she will be crowned and walk in the path of the Lord with the Lord. This poem lacks much of the extravagance of some of the others, and one is forced to consider the somewhat constricting influence of the octosyllabic couplet.

old Souldiers The Saints.
lustie Strong.
a privat seat i.e. make himself part of (the child).
breath . . . spent Dying for love of God.
poore six yeares She is only six years old.
pos'd Faced with.
nonage Childhood, immaturity.
Heates Passionate ideals.
the *Moors* Inhabitants of Spanish Morocco.
Diadem Crown.
Toyes Playthings.
Sweet not so fast i.e. child, don't act so precipitately.
Spouse Christ.
Brest's soft cabinet Poetic for 'bosom'.
uncase Rip out.
A Dart thrice dipt i.e. from one of the fiery seraphim, according to Teresa's vision.
To exercise their *Archerie* Note the image is the reverse of a Cupid's image, with the idea being that Teresa has been Divinely singled out for heavenly grace.
sweet *mansion* The body.
exhale to Heav'n at last i.e. be drawn up into heaven with your final breath.
reveal'd life i.e. God.
Deaths i.e. the wrongs she endured.
accompt . . . *Lamb's* An account of what you suffered for Christ.
rare *workes* The record of her goodness.

A Letter to the Countess of *Denbigh*

She was first Lady of the Bedchamber to Henrietta Maria and was converted to Catholicism. Crashaw's poem is an exhortation, but it is a poem of religion rather than of love – or, if you like, of religious love. The 'Irresolution' of the sub-title is told to go; the gate of bliss is religion, or more particularly Catholicism. The language is heavy with imagery, with analogies that are forced rather than natural; here the soul is compared to waters which become their own prisoners through frost; and the letter exhorts the receiver to look at the plenty of nature at harvest and seed-time, so that her own decision may be consonant with the laws of nature. The arguments for embracing Christ are here reinforced by the occasional climaxing line that is much longer in power and emphasis. The final urging is for her to yield to Christ, as she would to a lover.

Who grants at last Who gives in at the end.
strange Warrs This period of indecision.
his own Hands i.e. God's.
your brave Soul i.e. your commitment to religion.
Year takes cold In winter.
their own severer Shoar Cast upon the cold shore because they can't swim in their natural element.
the Pace you use Your slowness or hesitation.
Fruits answer Flowers i.e. fruits follow them – the implication is that she will reap the fruits of faith.
a stay Something that holds them back.
Doves . . . chast Loves i.e. these are symbols of chaste love.
grossest Metalls The crudest ore.
wo'ed Wooed, courted.
vouchsafe Give, grant.
Lightly as a Lambent Flame An echo of the Song of Solomon.
give Faith the Day i.e. allow faith to rule your heart.
before the Prize of Love i.e. lest you die before you have given complete love to God.
You're undone You won't be saved.

On Hope

The note appended to the poem in Helen Gardner's Penguin edition of *The Metaphysical Poets* is important, but if the student hasn't got this version in front of him, he perhaps needs some idea of what Cowley said. So some indication is given below, with a fuller treatment of Crashaw's reply. Cowley is particularly scathing about the existence of hope, which is ephemeral, merely a shadow; in fact hope is hopeless!

The verses are of ten lines, with a rhyme scheme of *aabbccddee*, the eighth line in each verse, whether Cowley's or Crashaw's, being shorter than the rest. Crashaw's reply to this initial condemnation is that hope is supreme on earth and in Heaven, and is in fact the 'entity' of what has not yet come about. Fate cannot harm Hope which is a 'Faire cloude of fire'. Cowley's reply to this is unequivocal – hope devours what it brings, so that happiness is sullied by the time it comes to us. Crashaw needs two verses to get back to this. The first is devoted to hope as a kind of blessing in marriage, and hope only dies in 'Love's full noone', just as sugar loses itself during fermentation in wine but becomes in fact the essence of the wine. Cowley responds with hope as the cheating lottery of fortune, and concentrates on its deceptive nature. Hope, retorts Crashaw, is beyond the earth, and is 'Our absent presence and our Future now'. Cowley considers hope to be the brother of fear, but Crashaw considers that hope is the sister of faith. The above summary cannot do justice to the tortuous nature of the poem or the dexterity (often spilling over into clever-clever innuendo) which characterizes this exercise – an extreme example of the art and artifice of metaphysical poetry.

misse Fail.

the hornes of Fates dilemma i.e. uncertainty.

hope . . . hopelesse Note the play on words characteristic of the method in this poem, and indeed in much metaphysical verse.

dowry The first of the marriage metaphors.

entity i.e. being (things we hope for exist in the future).

Subt'lest Cleverest.

Faire cloud of fire See Exodus, xiii,21–2.

a capacity i.e. you cannot be touched by fate.

thinne dilemma i.e. their puny uncertainty . . . (a contradiction of the argument used by Cowley).

estate . . . Legacies What you give you take away – note the contemporary imagery.

If it take ayre before Wine will turn to vinegar or will sour if it is exposed to air during fermentation.

Legacie . . . steward . . . Crown-lands Note that Crashaw immediately picks up the contemporary imagery used by Cowley and argues against it point by point.

Hopes . . . Than Spousall rites Hope does not wrong anyone, for marriage brings the hope of the joys of love.

taster i.e. a foretaste.

Loves full noone i.e. Hope only 'dies' when the full joy of love is actually being experienced.

Their subtile essence During fermentation the sugar is consumed by the yeast and converted into alcohol.

blankes i.e. worthless tickets.

drop . . . in tears i.e. it will rain.

ignes fatui Will o' the wisps.

kicks the curl'd heads . . . starres i.e. Hope is above the rule of the stars or Fate.

the fields of light, and love i.e. heaven.

Chymicks Chemists.

Anon i.e. soon (the discovery will be made).

hunted Nature The image is of a fox or other creature pursued – the other is that hope chases things but perhaps gets nowhere.

well-stay'd i.e. well made.

Temper'd i.e. balanced.

Queen Regent The idea is of Hope reigning.

Chymick . . . fugitive gold The alchemist and his search for the ideal distillation which will provide gold.

a glorious Huntresse Note again the reversion of the Cowley argument.

To our Lord, upon the Water made Wine

Christ turned water into wine at a marriage feast (John, ii,3–10) and this short poem is an exercise emanating from the beginning; but because of sin and suffering and perhaps the abuse of drink, tears flow, and thus wine has become water again.

The Weeper

This is Crashaw's hymn to Mary Magdalene. The verses are of six lines each, with alternate rhymes in the first four lines and the final pair of lines a rhyming couplet. The invocation is elaborately to her eyes, and the images reverberate for the first three verses. The next two are even more imaginative, with a cherub drinking Mary's tears for breakfast. And so it continues, with the poet ransacking the associations at will. Ultimately Angels come with Chrystall vialls to catch her tears, which are compared to wine. There is a temporary concern with her cheeks, but the poet returns to her eyes. No one must touch them, for 'The lamb hath dipt his white foot here'. He traces her following of Jesus. Her tears keep pace with her prayers; the time she mourned is given extended treatment, and gradually all leads to the feet of Christ, washed by Mary. It is impossible to gauge the sincerity of the poem, though the tone is certainly sustained and devotional. The imagery and the associations leave one, however, with the feeling of having taken part in a painful exercise with wit and ingenuity forming some kind of ritual in the poet's mind.

Sister Springs Her eyes.
spending Weeping.
Magdalen See Luke, viii, 2 and particularly John xx,11–18.
seed-time The first of the images to trace Mary's prolific weeping.
spangles Ornaments, stars.
milky Rivers The milky way.
Tastes of his breakefast Crashaw is here guilty of absurdity – in the minor metaphysicals this happens in the straining after analogy.
Balsome-sweating i.e. yielding medicinal resin (balsam).
coylie i.e. modesty.
the ease of i.e. releases, give comfort.
Balsom Balsam, i.e. comfort, soothing.
maiden Gemme i.e. the grape.
Angells with Chrystall Vialls Again the poet has fallen into absurdity.
Tagus The great Spanish river which reaches the Atlantic at Lisbon.
May i.e. blossom.
kind contrarieties i.e. the opposition of tears and smiles.
well pointed dart Love's, though here from Christ not Cupid.
avant! Go!
the Lamb The name given to Christ throughout the New Testament.
Galilean mountains i.e. around the Sea of Galilee.
unwelcome Unfriendly.
walking Baths ... Portable and compendious Oceans Note again the tipping over into absurdity.
a wandring mine/A voluntary mint Note again the extravagance of the image.
strowes Sheds.
tinct Tincture, essence.
Thou by tears Tears are seen here as a measurement of time because of the length of her grieving.
So doe perfumes expire Perfumes were extracted from flowers by heating, hence the 'unpittying fire' of this verse.
Aurora's **bed** i.e. that of the goddess of Dawn.
Prefer'd Dedicated to (the proud face of a mistress).
diadems Crowns.

Wishes. To his (supposed) Mistresse

This poem was published in *Delights of the Muses* in 1646. It is written in triplets and is a metaphysical exercise in ingenuity and wit, qualities of Crashaw that he was greatly tempted to display. The invocation is to an as-yet-unrevealed lady; at present she is his 'absent kisses'. He wishes her beauty that doesn't owe everything to outward show (i.e. dress and ornament). He is particularly insistent that she should be natural, not having a 'bought blush' or a 'set smile'. The only shop she should be made up from is that of nature. He then particularizes the various natural attributes she should possess. The catalogue tends to be repetitive; it is an extended exercise, but the poem gains little by the extension. In addition the lady must possess a 'well-tam'd heart' and of course she must be chaste. The only ironic note comes in the last line: 'Be ye my fictions; But her story.' This poem represents the elaborate metaphysical conceit without the elevation that it enjoyed in its greatest practitioners – Donne, Herbert and Marvell. This is a mannered poem, and on the whole rather dull.

shady leaves of Destiny i.e. hidden by fate.
Tire Dress (attire).
Taffata Taffeta; a stiff, glossy silk used then (and sometimes now), for ladies' ball gowns or other formal attire.
Tissew Light delicate silk or chiffon.
rampant feather Every now and then Crashaw succeeds in achieving the unexpected: here 'rampant' linked with 'feather'. The probable meaning is 'waving a lot in order to attract attention'.
Toyle From the French *toile*, one type of which would have been a light linen for women's summer dresses.
bought blush Cosmetics.
command the rest Rule in its own right.
sets ope Sets up, following on 'shop' in the previous line.
Pen of Truth i.e. what is natural and real.
ru'th Possibly 'rueth' – rues; i.e. the reader regrets (rues) the passing of her/his own once clear young cheek.
Boxe i.e. of perfumes or cosmetics.
carry nothing thence away i.e. no disease.
oppress/Their richest Tires i.e. looks which are superior to anything worn.
displaces i.e. are better than, brighter than, diamonds.
wanton Day Luxuriant light.
Bee its own blush i.e. because it is so inferior to her.

noble smart Feelings.

pay lesse Arrowes i.e. are modest, discreet and chaste.

bin Been (have been).

fond and flight i.e. flutterings of a natural kind when the bridegroom comes for her (Crashaw is the least sexual of the metaphysicals; there is something coy and a little unwholesome about all this).

are Day all Night i.e. everything she does is pure and reasonable.

Welcome Friend i.e. her mind will be on spiritual things too.

Sydnaean **showers** A nice compliment to Sir Philip Sidney, noted for the sweetness of his conversation.

old Winters head Age.

lowres Which causes melancholy.

Downe Softness, perfect sleep.

Her counsell Keeping herself to herself.

poore/Of wishes i.e. unhealthy desires.

And I wish – No more And so does the reader.

just Bayes i.e. her laurels may provide me with mine (through my verse).

uncloath Lay bare.

My fancies My imaginings.

fictions . . . story Fine balance to end the poem.

Revision questions on Richard Crashaw

1 Consider Crashaw's treatment of either Mary Magdalene or St Teresa in the poem dedicated to the praise of one of them.

2 Write an essay on the specifically metaphysical facets of Crashaw's work.

3 What claims has Crashaw to be considered a fine lyrical poet? You should refer to one or two poems, or parts of poems, in your answer.

4 In what ways do you find Crashaw's poetry either cloying or absurd? You should refer to one or two poems in your answer.

5 'Unfelt exercises in verse.' How far would you agree or disagree with this comment on Crashaw's poetry?

John Donne
(1572–1631)

The poet and his work

John Donne, the third child in a family of six, was born in Bread Street, London. His father was a member of the Ironmongers' Company and his mother, a Catholic, was the daughter of John Heywood and a great-niece of Sir Thomas More. In her Donne witnessed the Catholicism he was first to embrace and later reject. After his father's death in 1576 his mother made a prosperous second marriage to a physician, John Syminges. During the next few years three of Donne's sisters died.

In 1584 Donne matriculated at Hart Hall, Oxford, and it seems likely that he spent some time at Cambridge later in the 1580s, following this up with foreign travel. His mother, again a widow, married a prominent Catholic gentleman, and in May 1592 Donne entered Lincoln's Inn. He remained there for two or three years, then joined the Earl of Essex's expedition to Cadiz in 1596, setting out from Plymouth; his status was that of gentleman. He took part in the sacking of Cadiz and in the following year accompanied the expedition to the Azores. Shortly after his return he entered the service of Sir Thomas Egerton, Lord Keeper of England, and this enabled him to become a Member of Parliament in 1601. In the latter part of the same year he secretly married Ann More, daughter of Sir George More and Egerton's niece; for this he was imprisoned in the Fleet prison and lost his post with Sir Thomas Egerton. He was freed, however, when the marriage was pronounced valid.

In the next three years three children were born to the Donnes, a fourth arriving in 1607. Further children followed, two of them still-born. Donne began to publish verse and prose and to help in writing against the Catholic Church. He was urged to take Holy Orders, but initially considered himself unworthy. In 1614 two of his children died and in the following year he was ordained. By 1616 he had become Reader at Lincoln's Inn and had preached before the Queen. His wife died in 1617, aged 33, shortly after giving birth to another still-born child.

In 1618 Donne preached at Court, and in 1619 in Europe. In 1621 he was elected Dean of St Paul's. The next few years saw the steady publication of his sermons, and he continued as a fashionable and dedicated preacher. In 1630, however, he was taken ill, and in February 1631 preached his last sermon in the Chapel at Whitehall; shortly afterwards he insisted on a drawing being made of him in his shroud. He died on 31 March and was buried in St Paul's.

Unbeknown to himself, Donne sired a school of poetry. In the words of the poet Thomas Carew (1594/5–1640): 'Here lies a king, that ruled as hee thought fit,/The universal monarchy of wit.' Yet even this is inadequate, for Donne altered the language of poetry by linking science, mathematics, abstract thought, geographical discovery, Christian and pagan thought with the colloquial, the passionate, the sensual and the grotesque. Strangely, the young man of licence and the older man of fearing and fearsome faith are also linked: in the audacious hyperbole, and in the unexpected turns that mark the major poet of feeling and intellect in our language. Donne is never dull: punning, elaborating a conceit, cursing or battering himself, his intuitive poetry amazes and delights.

Poem summaries, textual notes and revision questions
Aire and Angels

Angels are spirits but visible as 'bodies' of air. In effect this poem is in the form of two sonnets, but they are far from regular, having varied rhythmic lines and a rhyme scheme that has a triplet instead of a couplet at the end. Again we appreciate the technical ingenuity of the poet. In the first 'sonnet' he compares the effect of his beloved to that of an angel. Now, however, she has become more substantial and his love is directed by his senses, for love cannot exist through the soul alone. The second 'sonnet' shows him almost 'overturned' by the impact of her physical beauty. From here on the argument becomes more abstract, with the poet anxious for her love to be a recursion of his own, but this must be both physical and spiritual. Again the control throughout the poem is admirable, but the obscurity of the last section, with its overtly metaphysical arguments requiring some knowledge of scholastic theology if it is to be clearly understood, makes this a poem where the conceit inherent in the title and the complex brilliance of the presentation detract from an immediate response.

Some lovely glorious nothing The angelic quality, the divine essence of being, which cannot be seen.

limmes of flesh i.e. the physical response to what he sees through his senses.

subtile Cunning.

ballast Note that this connects with the image of the pinnace that follows.

wares i.e. what she has to offer, her physical appeal, which threatens to overcome him.

nor in nothing ... can love inhere Love cannot exist in these things (and nothings).

not pure ... yet pure Air is clear, but not as ethereally clear as spirits.

spheare i.e. the element in which love may exist and prosper.

Just such disparitie i.e. the difference between the love of a woman and the love of a man is like the difference between pure spirit (angel) and air. Thus the conceit has been worked through.

The Anniversarie

A poem in three ten-line verses, with the last four lines rhyming alternately and the rest of the poem in couplets. The analogy with the outer world in the passing of a year is deliberately drawn, and there is a springing optimism in the poet's feeling that their love 'hath no decay'. It is unlike earthly things, is the implication, for it is immortal. Death divorces the body from the soul, but their souls after death will leave their graves and thus lovers will be united. The final verse celebrates their blessedness in heaven with all other souls of like capacity, and then returns to their earthly state, the analogy with Kings and Princes being developed and the conceit extended to embrace the 'reign' of their love. The tone is intimate and warm, the microcosmic emphasis is again strong, as we see through the imagery referred to immediately above.

Running ... first, last, everlasting Note that all the stress is on the *permanence* despite the changes in time, or life and death.

inmates Lodgers, i.e. not permanently present.

prove Demonstrate, show (the increase of their love).

soules from their graves i.e. the souls leaving the bodies.

refraine (Let us) stop any doubts.

The Apparition

This poem of rejection is couched in bitter rhetorical language, although it treats of a subject enamoured of the court poets of the time. But the conceit goes beyond rejection and has a forward look into the degradation to come for the false mistress. His ghost will see her in bed with a lover who, thinking she wants him to make love again, will shrink from her. This is what she will have been reduced to. Because of this she will be more a ghost – rejected by her lover – than the poet is. What he will say then he keeps hidden from her now. The colloquial tone throughout is cynical, imaginative and unsparing, and the result is an effective picture which is true to reality – an essential truth of what happens, expressed with verve and bitterness.

fain'd vestall Fake virgin, which is what she has pretended to be to her new lover.
sicke taper i.e. the candle or light will tremble at the presence of the foreign body – the ghost.
Aspen wretch i.e. trembling like an aspen tree.
A veryer ghost i.e. more of a ghost from apprehension or fear than the poet is.
threatenings i.e. of retribution for her having been untrue to him.

The Calme

This is written in 1597 on the expedition to the Azores; it is again in couplets.

The calm at sea signifies the failure of the ships of Raleigh and Essex to put the Spanish fleet out of action. There is a running comparison at the beginning with the storms which have passed, but the wit and innuendoes take in 'ended playes', while the fleet is unflatteringly compared to an old clothes shop. There is thus a certain self-mockery in the tone of the poem, which conveys admirably the impotence of the becalmed fleet. There is no escaping the situation; comparisons with Bajazet (in Marlowe's *Tamburlaine*) and with Samson indicate the range of Donne's innuendo. The last lines of the poem convey the fact that fate, here epitomized by the calm, is something from which they could not pray to be relieved, but after asserting that man is as nothing, Donne paradoxically indicates that his capacity to feel misery is an underlining of his individuality and power.

One can easily appreciate the popularity of this poem, with its contemporary allusions; the immediacy of the experience and its attendant frustrations is finely evoked.

The fable is inverted . . . a storke before A reference to one of Aesop's Fables where the frogs ask for a King and get a log. Dissatisfied, they ask again, later to find that their King is to be a stork who eats them up.

thy mistresse glasse i.e. her mirror.

trimme Sails.

Like courts removing Note the economy of the image, which yet shows the poet aware of home.

seamens ragges Washing.

frippery Shop for old clothes.

lanthornes Lanterns.

Earths hollownesses i.e. where the winds are set free.

lost friends . . . sought foes An indication of the failure of the expedition and the splitting of the fleets of Raleigh and Essex.

Calenture Tropical fever in which seamen are suffering from the hallucination that the sea is a green field, into which they jump.

walkers in hot Ovens Another reference to Shadrach, Meshach and Abednego. See note on 'Children in th'oven' in 'Satyre: of Religion', p. 51.

Bajazet Conquered by Tamburlaine in Marlowe's *Tamburlaine the Great*; he is imprisoned in a cage.

Sampson Samson lost his outstanding strength when, betrayed by Delilah, his seven locks of hair were cut off. See Judges, xiv–xvi.

Ants . . . Snake invade A reference to the pet of the Emperor Tiberius which was eaten by ants.

finny chips i.e. thin pieces of wood.

bed-ridde ships i.e. they are becalmed. A striking metaphor; this and the following six lines epitomize the frustration of stagnation.

'gainst which wee all forget to pray i.e. the one thing happens that we haven't bargained for.

The Canonization

The title refers directly to those who are made saints because they have martyred themselves for love. The tone is ironic and impatient, critical of those who might object to his loving. The shape of each verse is the same, with lines one, four, eight and nine rhyming, a couplet in the first four lines and a triplet as lines five to seven. The tone is self-mocking as well as ironic, for he urges people to get on with their own particular concerns and not pay any attention to his. In the second verse he asserts that he is injuring no one by his love, either in the physical or the legal sense; verse three idealizes the lovers as being symbolic of power (the eagle) and gentleness (the dove), but this does not seem complete enough to the poet, who compares them to the phoenix, which is unique and has the capacity for self renewal in its own destruction. This is perhaps the most elaborate of the conceits here. The lovers will survive anyway, he says, in verse ('We'll build in sonnets pretty rooms') and through these 'hymnes' they will be canonized.

The last verse looks into the future, with the lovers being invoked by later generations as 'A Patterne', the perfect love which others cannot attain because of their own natures. We are reminded, as with the 'well wrought urne' of the previous verse, of Petrarch and Laura. Not the least ingenious quality of the poem is the number of rhymes and half-rhymes used to complement the repeated 'love'.

chide my palsy i.e. the implication that he is too old (to have an unwise affair).

a course A means of advancement.

honour . . . grace i.e. legal or titled dignitaries.

the Kings reall . . . stamped face i.e. the real living King or his representation on his coins.

ships . . . teares . . . forward spring All marks of the external world unaffected by their love.

plaguie Bill i.e. the list of deaths issued every day during a plague.

Litigious men i.e. those engaged in legal battles.

another flye,/We'are Tapers too i.e. burnt by our own flames of passion.

the'Eagle and the Dove The first is equated with power, the second with softness, meekness.

Phoenix ridle hath more wit Is more suitable – see the summary of this poem above.

Wee dye and rise the same i.e. come to our consummation, and then make love again.

a well wrought urne A funeral urn with representations of the lovers on it.

The greatest ashes i.e. eminent people who have died.

Into the glasses i.e. so that you could only take account of worldly things.

epitomize i.e. seemed to be everything.

A patterne of your love Other less happy lovers are told to model their love on this one.

The Dreame

Three verses of ten lines each, with a short third line and a climaxing couplet at the end of each verse. The poet is woken from a sensual dream by the reality of the beloved, and promptly expresses the wish that they should consummate now what had been his fantasy. The second verse further elaborates on her timely arrival and the fact that she has seen into the substance of what he was dreaming. Now that he is out of the dream he has doubts; but he feels that she will go and come again despite all, and as long as he feels that she will, he has hope; without it he would rather die.

For reason i.e. consonant with being awake rather than asleep and dreaming.
let's do the rest i.e. let's make love.
though saw'st my heart i.e. you read exactly what I was feeling and thinking in my dream.
cam'st to kindle i.e. to wake me into love.

Elegie: His Picture

The elegies are thought to be early poems written in the 1590s, but their licentiousness and sensuality caused them to be banned; some were not printed until 1635. This brief one, published in 1633, is, like the previous poem, written in couplets varied in pauses and rhythms. The conceit developed is that the portrait bequeathed to his mistress will survive whereas he may not; 'I dead' it will be, so to speak, living. The poet is setting out on a journey and may, if he is not harmed permanently, return with the marks of suffering, or even physical wounds, upon him. But the portrait will be unchanged, its delicacy the reminder of the man he once was.

take my Picture i.e. a miniature; these were much in vogue as gifts.
shadowes i.e ghosts, spirits, but with a pun on the 'shadow' of the portrait, which is a likeness.
cares rash sodaine hoariness i.e. hair whitened overnight by worry.
powders blew staines i.e. made by the gunpowder.
taxe Criticize.
This shall say what I was The picture will tell its own truth.
That which in him The lines mean that he was once delicate and fine, but that he has now been roughened by hardship.

disus'd Not accustomed to.

Elegie: On his Mistris

This elegy, first published in 1635, tells of the poet's first meeting with his mistress and the ensuing results. Again the form is the couplet, but this is essentially dramatic narrative, with a certain tension maintained through references to rivals, spies and the parents' anger. His mistress even has to accompany him disguised as his page in order to conceal their love from the prying eyes of the world. While he is away from her now though he will 'Thirst to come back'. A typical metaphysical conceit has the poet imagining his beloved's death while he is absent from her; then his soul will seek hers out.

The succeeding image is a classical one – another staple Donne device – and this is reinforced by another often present in Donne, namely, 'That absent lovers one in th'other bee'. The poet then urges his mistress to be what she is, to assume no disguises. He goes on to list the masks that hide reality: men apeing others, men of fashion, and those who would uncover her disguise and take sexual advantage of her. He outlines the risks she will take if she travels with him, and urges her, therefore, to remain in England, to dream happily of him, rejecting nightmares of what may befall him.

remorse Here the meaning is compassion (rather than regret for a wrong one has committed).

divorcement Separation.

Boreas In Greek myth, the north wind.

Orithea The nymph carried off by Boreas, with whom she lived contentedly, bearing him children; Donne here appears to be twisting the story for his own ends.

to have prov'd/Dangers unurg'd i.e. to have undertaken or subjected oneself to danger when there was no need.

Richly cloth'd Apes People who ape others are easily discovered and seen through.

Camelions They resemble chameleons, small lizards that change colour to adapt to any background. This is the beginning of an indictment against the hypocrisy of the French.

Spittles i.e. hospitals. The implication is that French men of fashion are venereally diseased.

knowe thee, 'and knowe thee i.e. recognize you and, accordingly, have you (sexually).

indifferent i.e. ready to have boy or woman.

As Lots faire guests were vext See Genesis, xix,1–7; the Sodomites tried to ravish the angels Lot was entertaining, thinking they were young men.

spungie hydroptique i.e. sodden with drink. (Donne uses the word 'hydroptique' elsewhere to imply excessive thirst, even using the word 'dropsy' in the same way, whereas 'hydropsy' and 'dropsy' both mean an excess of fluid in the body tissues.)

gallerie i.e. the room where those waiting to see the King or Queen were placed.

Our greate King i.e. God.

Alpes i.e. in Switzerland or Italy.

Assayld, fight, taken Note here the splendid single word effects which provide a graphic and imaginative (and imaginary) story of their own.

Augure me i.e. hope for me, prophesy for me.

Jove The chief of the Roman gods.

Elegie: To his Mistris Going to Bed

Banned from the 1633 edition, this first appeared in 1669. Again the chosen mode is the couplet, and the frank colloquial sensuality of the opening moves into the military/sexual language and innuendoes of the third and fourth lines. The poem is tense with expectation, even lust, so that an atmosphere of intimacy is subtly blended with one of voyeurism and striptease. The movement is pleasurable, sensual and self-mocking, the latter delightfully conveyed through a kind of inverted use of the pastoral convention in such lines as 'As when from flowery meades th'hills shadow steales', which is an obvious poeticism usually employed to convey an artificial rather than the real experience implied here.

The references to Angels are quickly followed by the sensual associations of 'Mahomets Paradise', while ghosts are compared, since they raise hairs of fear, to nudity, which raises the male sexual organ.

The second verse paragraph is redolent of sensual indulgence and enables the poet to introduce one of his favourite images ('Oh my America, my new found lande') together with another, the 'myne of precious stones'. Women are compared to 'mystique books' which men 'read' when they are revealed (unclothed). Again there is a classical reference, here to Atalanta, and the haste for consummation is finely conveyed in the concluding couplet.

labour ... in labour i.e. strive for a sexual climax ... am impatient.

standing i.e. in erection.

heavens zone Orion.

spangled brest-plate The stomacher which covered the bosom and was ornamented with stones.

harmonious chime Ladies at this time wore chiming watches.

buske 'Busk', a strip of rigid material covering a corset front.

wyrie coronet Her corset.

hairy dyadem Pubic hair.

Mahomets Paradise i.e. bliss.

Ill spirits Evil angels.

the flesh upright i.e. the male erection.

Empiree Lands rules by an emperor.

Then where my hand is set Note the combination here of the legal agreement (perhaps marriage) and the fact that his hand is placed where he will shortly enter her.

Atalanta's balls According to the Greek myth, Hippomenes outwitted Atalanta. She had undertaken to marry the suitor who could beat her in a race. As he ran, Hippomenes dropped three golden apples given to him by Venus; Atalanta picked them up and lost the race. Donne has cunningly reversed the myth.

wee ... imputed grace ... dignify i.e. we are the lucky chosen few.

as to a midwife i.e. have no false modesty. Perhaps also a forward, ironic look to the result of their consummation – a child.

more covering than a man A clever punning association – she needs no clothes since she is to be 'covered' by the body of her lover.

The Expiration

Two six-line verses, a quatrain of alternate lines rhyming in each, followed by a couplet. The title has a dual meaning: a breathing-out, and a letting go of life, which second idea includes the separation of the two lovers by parting, itself a kind of death – a favourite image of Donne's. The poem embodies wordplay and punning.

benight i.e. darken (with the thought of parting).

kil'd ... death ... murderer ... double dead Note the repetitive emphasis which so effectively conveys the anguish of parting.

The Extasie

The title of the poem is rooted in a religious experience of a mystical nature in which some aspect of heavenly truth is shown.

Here Donne turns the concept into an individual expression of the deeper revelations of the truths of love. The lovers are in a conventional pastoral setting and gazing absorbedly at each other. They see the image in each other's eyes, and their souls leave their bodies; anyone watching them would become more pure as a result of their experience. The lovers discover through this 'Extasie' that it was not merely sexual attraction that called forth their love but the various elements of which love is made, and an analogy is drawn with the transplanted violet, which multiplies. The single soul emerges from the two commingled and overcomes all doubts. The lovers know how this soul has come about, and they know too the relationship between their souls and their bodies. It was the body that first conveyed love to us through sense perception and experience, for what is spiritual – the soul – has to come through the fleshly medium of experience. And just as we try to create the fusion of souls or spirits, so the body provides the starting-point for the inception of love between man and woman. To neglect the body is to imprison it, and even those who disbelieve this cannot doubt the evidence of their senses as conveyed through the body. And when our souls return to our bodies, little or no change will be apparent.

A Pregnant banke The traditional pastoral scene given subtle metaphysical twists.

violets Symbolic of faith in love.

a fast balme i.e. certain and unwavering, as if stuck with gum.

entergraft Hold and entwine.

pictures . . . propagation i.e. the reflection of the other was all they were making, as distinct from making physical love.

All day . . . all the day Note that the effect of repetition finely conveys time.

concoction i.e. the finest essence extracted by fire, purifying. This runs into the sense of the next line.

unperplex Make clear what was obscure.

what did move What set them going.

severall Individual, separate.

poore, and scant i.e. weak and spindly in growth.

That abler soule . . . Defects of loneliness controuls i.e. the fusion of the two souls has increased their power over their limits.

whom no change can invade The 'new' soul has been created and cannot be changed or be subject to change.

they the spheare i.e. they represent the physical manifestation of ourselves complete in our souls.

sense . . . Nor are drosse to us, but allay i.e. our bodies provide the sense perceptions, but they are not decayed to us but a mixture (alloy) of good and lower things.

Soe soule into the soule ... to body first repaire The coming together of the souls may be first engendered in the coming together of the bodies of the lovers.

As our blood labours A direct reference to metaphysics, where spirits are produced by the blood.

subtile i.e. clever, skilful and supple.

So must pure lovers We must return to our bodies (here personified as a Prince) and display our feelings by using them, i.e. making love.

Weake men i.e. those responding to the demands of the flesh. Perhaps even those who need the assurance of the flesh in order to believe in love.

dialogue of one i.e. because their souls are mingled and have become one.

when we'are to bodies gone i.e. (love will change but little) when we are responding to our bodies.

The Flea

This is Donne's treatment of one of the commonplaces, sometimes scurrilous, of love poetry in the sixteenth century. Fleas suck the blood of the beloved – that is their consummation; hence the starting point for the comparison with man, who desires the access to his mistress's body which the flea has already obtained. The poem is in three verses, cunningly shaped to include the climaxing triplet at the end of each of the three. Note particularly the idea of the mingling of bloods as symbolizing a true marriage. In the second verse the man begs his mistress not to kill the flea; in so doing she would be in part killing herself and him, since the flea having bitten them both, contains a mingling of their blood. However, in the third verse, the woman kills the flea.

mariage temple Note the spiritual connotations of this phrase.

cloysterd Again there is a religious association.

Though use The idea of the flea, the man and the mistress being indivisible here, and associations too with the holy trinity.

Just so much honor You will lose as little by yielding as the flea actually took from you.

Good Friday 1613. Riding Westward

This was obviously composed during the journey from Polesworth to Montgomery on Good Friday 1613. It is written in couplets, most of which are end-stopped, thus indicating the serious meditative quality the poem possesses. Man is moved by devotion but is subject to external influences; so we are sometimes deflected by events from single-minded movement towards God or Christ, just as on this journey the poet's soul is moving one way and his body another. He then, because of the day, ponders on Christ's death and resurrection. It was like death itself to see God die and it is almost too much for the poet to contemplate. His mind tries to take in the terrible image of the crucifixion, and his imagination ranges freely over the degradation of it. From then on he contemplates the sufferings of the Virgin Mary. Although his back is to his Saviour, he asks to be scourged for his own sins. When his true self emerges he will turn and face Christ.

Let mans Soule be a Spheare The analogy is developed over the first six lines: briefly, the spheres are influenced by other spheres, just as man is influenced by events and occasions – here with the poet riding westward.

my Soules forme bends towards the East i.e. he is moved towards Christ (though physically he is going in the opposite direction).

a Sunne Here symbolizing Christ as well as the actual sun – an obvious pun.

Who sees Gods face . . . must dye See Exodus, xxiii,20.

Lieutenant Nature shrinke Nature was disturbed when Christ was crucified.

his footstoole crack See Matthew, xxviii for the earthquake reference.

the Sunne winke Refers to the darkness that covered the earth as Christ died.

Zenith to us A good example of Donne's imaginative range, for God is the highest wherever one is.

God's partner here i.e. the Virgin Mary.

That thou may'st know mee i.e. see in me your image and that I have come to serve you again.

The Good-Morrow

The abrupt colloquial opening is characteristic of Donne, its anti-romantic rhetoric in fact concealing the idea that the dream of the beloved was the only reality possible to him before they 'loved'. Again there are three verses, here of seven lines each, the first part forming a quatrain, with the triplet at the end once more providing a rounding-off climax. The second verse explores the completeness of love, the 'good-morrow' indicating the new rich life they have in one another both spiritually and physically. And just as the first verse embodies the far-fetched reference to the 'seaven sleepers den', so the second is rich in contemporary reference which gives immediacy to their love and confers upon it a microcosmic intensity. The 'world' image is continued in the last verse; again there is the use of rhetorical question, and the idea of 'two loves be one', central to the poem, is further emphasized.

troth Truth

wean'd ... suck'd ... countrey pleasures Note the childish images which represent the past, or immature love as distinct from their mature sexuality now.

the seaven sleepers den Seven Christians persecuted by the Emperor Decius in the 3rd century AD were reputed to have slept for some two hundred years.

watch not one another out of feare i.e. the souls contemplate each other not in the sense of checking up, but because they are delighting completely in their own love.

one little roome, an every where Note the microcosmic effect of this; it is a favourite emphasis of Donne's.

Maps i.e. of the heavens.

each hath one, and is one Though each is an individual, their love makes them complete in each other and therefore one.

What ever dyes, was not mixt equally A love that dies is one where the two did not love each other with equal strength.

none doe slacken i.e. lose the strength of their love.

Holy Sonnets: Divine Meditations

There is considerable doubt about the order and time of these poems, though Helen Gardner takes the view that they were probably written in 1609. These sonnets are conventional in form, even to the number of syllables to the line.

1 The octave has two quatrains in which the 1st and 4th, 5th and 8th have the same rhyme, as do the 2nd, 3rd, 6th and 7th. The sestet has a similar *abba* rhyme, and the climaxing couplet consists of a double rhyme. The octave affirms that the poet was made for God, to serve him, and that the blood of Christ has purchased that service. In the sestet he is aware that he is succumbing to the temptations of Satan; he calls upon God to

fight for him to save his soul from the devil. This is the theme of many of Donne's Divine Poems.

many titles i.e. dues (to God).
decay'd Sinful.
sonne ... shine Note the deliberate pun.
I betray'd Succumbed to temptation (of the devil).
worke i.e. because you have made me, I am your 'worke'.
lov'st ... chuse ... hates ... lose Note the careful antithetical balance of these words, an equivalent to the balance between good and evil.

2 This is in the same form as the previous sonnet. It begins with an invocation to the poet's 'black Soule' which is now to face the onset of death. Various analogies are drawn with the corrupt soul, the last in the octave being that of a thief dragged to prison and execution. In the sestet the poet considers the question of grace, and in the vivid language we have come to associate with him considers that it can only be obtained by the cleansing process of washing in Christ's blood.

turne Return, go back.
hal'd Hauled.
But who shall give Note the rhetorical question.
red ... dyes ... white Note the vivid physical effects of the spiritual experience.

3 Note particularly the apposite playhouse imagery for this sonnet, again in the same form in terms of rhyme and the division of octave and sestet. Another dramatic utterance at the point of death, with the casting away of sins as the soul takes flight for heaven, but always with the fear that it may not arrive there.

playes last scene The young Donne would of course have been a frequenter of the Elizabethan playhouse.
pilgrimages i.e. journey through life.
unjoynt Divorce, separate.
shall see that face i.e. of God at the Day of Judgement.
Impute me righteous i.e. allow me to be accepted as righteous now that I have purged myself of my sins.

4 The same form as the other sonnets in this sequence, with the theme of repentance to the fore. The first part invokes the recall of the bodies scattered around the earth, but then the poet considers that his sins are greater than all these, regardless of how they have died. Only by learning to repent in life will the poet be pardoned for his sins.

the round earth's imagin'd corners See Revelation, vii,1.
flood . . . fire Note the complete contrast, the Deluge of the past and the Fire which will bring about the end of the world in the future.
abound i.e. are measured more than.
lowly ground i.e. earth, in life.

5 This is almost an argument against his own damnation because he is a man: only mankind, not lesser things, can be damned. Why cannot I have the mercy of God? The sestet finds the poet abjectly condemning himself for daring to challenge God, saying that his tears may drown his sins, which he hopes that God will be merciful enough to forget.

intent or reason Will, and the ability to think and judge.
worthy blood The blood of Christ.
heavenly Lethean A combination of the pagan and the Christian, since Lethe is the river of Hades, the river of oblivion.
though wilt forget i.e. my sins.

6 Death is directly invoked here in a magnificent rhetorical opening which sounds the note of Donne's later sermons. The quatrain establishes the immortality of the soul against which death is powerless. If rest and sleep are images of death, since they give pleasure, death must yield correspondingly greater pleasure. Again, our best people die young, and death is merely a slave waiting on the various events that lead to it. The immortality of the soul is effectively the death of death. This is a finely economical sonnet, rich in single word effects, with a sustained personification of 'Death' throughout giving it a curiously triumphant tone.

pictures Images.
soules delivery i.e. the freedom of the soul when the body dies.
poppie This produces sleep because it contains opium.
charmes Sleep-inducing spells.

Holy Sonnet

'Batter my heart, three person'd God . . .' is in the same form as the other sonnets. It is charged with self-indictment, with a fine military image of the 'usurpt towne' indicating the inroads made by the devil into the heart of the poet. The sestet contains some of Donne's most typical imagery, in that the prison/ravish/divorce/enthrall statements show that the holy sonnets and the earlier poems have a shared body of images and that the passion of a sexual nature has here been transmuted, though in like language, to spiritual passion.

three person'd i.e. the Holy Trinity.
knocke . . . shine . . . mend . . . blowe, burn and make me new Notice the perfect balancing of these images, almost likening God to a blacksmith.
Nor ever chast, except you ravish mee An audacious image for a religious poem.

Holy Sonnet

'Since she whome I lovd, hath payd her last debt'. This is a moving poem written after the death of his wife Ann in child-birth in 1617. The poet says that now his wife is dead he will devote himself entirely to religion. His wife had given the impetus to his spiritual feelings, and though he has found God he is consumed by thirst. God seeks out his soul to unite it with that of his wife now in heaven, but he fears that he may give his love either to saints or to earthly things, or again to the devil.

payd . . . debt/To Nature, and to hers i.e. paid her debt to mortality, and to her family.
shew the head i.e. reveal where they spring from.
dropsy i.e. unslaked thirst, wish for much drink. (See note, p.36, on 'spungie, hydroptique' in 'Elegie: On his Mistris'.)
putt thee out i.e. overcome God's influence.

A Hymne to Christ, at the Authors last going into Germany

Donne went to Germany as a chaplain in 1619, the occasion of this poem. All he does, says the poet, will be in the service of Christ. He yields up his homeland to Christ, saying that he leaves all in His service, though the third verse is critical of God, returning in the fourth to the dismissal of all worldly things to enter the everlasting night, which is death.

The four verses are of eight lines each, with rhyming couplets and one unrhymed line (line 7).

this Iland England.

thy sea i.e. the blood of Christ.

in my winter i.e. my old age.

an harmonious Soul i.e. one who is living in concord with his soul and in devotion to his religion.

takes libertie i.e. stops us from loving someone else (other than Christ).

Fame, Wit Donne is looking back to his early years and considers these personifications 'false mistresses'.

goe out of sight i.e. a long way from home.

An Everlasting night Undoubtedly death, in view of Donne's morbid repetitions that he may not survive a voyage.

A Hymne to God the Father

Three verses of six lines each with alternate lines rhyming and a much shorter last line, which is a repeated refrain in these verses indicating the magnitude of his sin. Again it was probably written during the poet's illness in 1623. There is a subtle punning on his own name throughout.

where I begunne i.e. the sin of man through Adam.

thou hast not done The number of my sins is not complete, nor have you got me, John Donne.

thy Sunne i.e. Christ.

Thou hast done i.e. my sins are gold, and you have me in death.

Hymne to God my God, in my sicknesse

Commentators vary in their dating of this poem, which belongs either to Donne's illness of 1623 or to his final one. The poem is in the form of six five-line verses with alternate lines rhyming; it is ironic in tone, with a dry appraisal of the death-bed scene, albeit his own.

The first verse is characterized by a musical analogy, the second by Donne's favourite medical/geographical image; the third continues this theme and includes the Resurrection at the end. Verse four ranges geographically again, verse five is strongly biblical, hence spiritual, and the final verse confirms this. The poem is typical of Donne in tone, conceit, wit, analogy and sheer range of inventive association.

Cosmographers Map-makers of the cosmos (universe), but here their maps are of Donne's body.
South-west discoverie i.e. death.
Per fretum febris By the heat of fever.
West i.e. death.
yeeld return to none i.e. there is no going back.
West and East ... are one i.e. through death and Christ, the beginning of the Resurrection.
Jerusalem i.e. heaven or Paradise, and the following references are attempting to give it a local habitation and a name.
Anyan Probably Annam.
Magellan i.e. the straits dividing South America and Tierra del Fuego.
Gibraltare The rock at the entrance to the Mediterranean.
Japhet ... Cham ... Sem Noah's sons.
Paradise Thought to be near Damascus.
both *Adams* In view of what follows, Christ is the other Adam.
purple The blood of Christ.
his thornes i.e. the crown of thorns.

Loves Alchymie

The poet asserts that many who have known more about love than he does say they've found where its essential happiness lies, but no matter how much he has loved or will love in the future it still eludes him. Just as every alchemist glorifies his own elixir as the one which will cure all the ills of life, so lovers dream of a like perfection but do not discover it. The second 12-line verse begins with the rhetorical question: can a man be as happy in love as he, the poet, is without? People find what they want in love, a marriage of minds, or the sexual enjoyment of the first day, often accompanied by coarse jests and music. The last couplet is cynical; you will not find intelligence or intellect in women, merely sweetness and wit. They are dead flesh to be used for sexual pleasure, though the last word of the poem 'possest' may mean that they are sometimes in the grasp of a spirit, and an evil one at that.

love, get, tell Note the thrust in the repetition, suggestive of sexual virility.
imposture i.e. fake, pretentious.
chymique Alchemist.

Elixar i.e. the substance which would cure all ills.
pregnant pot i.e. potent mixtures.
winter-seeming summers night i.e. brief and cold happiness.
Bubles Trifles.
short scorne i.e. the haste of the bridegroom to enjoy the bride.
rude hoarse minstralsey i.e. the marriage celebrations, sometimes held
  outside the bedroom of the married couple.
Mummy Dead flesh.
possest Enjoyed, kept; alternatively possessed by frenzy or a (possibly
  evil) spirit.

Loves Deitie

Four verses of seven lines each, with alternate lines rhyming in
the first four, followed by a triplet. The last line of each verse is a
variant of the same thought, and acts as a kind of refrain. The
theme is the common one of the poet being scorned by the
woman he loves. He refers back to the god of love; surely his
function was to bring together those who responded to each
other. Hence it cannot be love in his own case until his love is
returned. But modern times have debased the currency of the
god of love, and everything passes for love. In the final verse the
lover comes to the conclusion that if the recipient of his love
should return it, that might be even worse than his present
plight; for she loves another and would so be inconstant.

Who dyed before us i.e. died before conventions of love were
  established.
which did scorne i.e. who rejected him.
a destinie i.e. a way of loving.
vice-nature, custome Which our inverted nature accepts as the mode
  of doing things.
even Corresponding.
office Function.
fit/Actives to passives Suit lovers who declared their love to those who
  responded to it.
Correspondencie Compatibility, mutual love.
To rage . . . This is mockery of the way poets employ conventional
  phrases in their verses to their mistresses.
purlewe Purlieu: territory.

Loves Growth

Another poem in the form of two sonnets, though with varying length of line, having some alternate lines rhyming and some couplets, with the climactic couplet rounding off each section. The poet's contemplation of his own love, its growth and the various influences which contribute to it, includes mockery of those who write about love as an abstraction, without knowledge of, or feeling for, it except in the form of verbal expression. The second verse examines the growth of love in the spring, the imagery drawing on nature, the sun, indeed the universe: all things being 'concentric unto thee'. The microcosmic turn continues; the aside in which he notes that princes who are granted tax increases in wartime retain them when peace returns links the natural and human world, for the increase in love experienced by the poet will also be retained in spite of seasonal changes or the changes that time brings.

Loves Growth Note the sexual implication of the title.
so pure Firm and unchanging.
Vicissitude i.e. changes in fortune or in time, just as the grass changes according to the season.
quintessence The essential thing, the basic purity.
mixt of all stuffes, paining A combination of all things which worry.
working vigour Driving force, sexual power.
Mistresse but their Muse i.e. who write poems to an imaginary woman not a real one, the expression of the poem being more important than anything else.
being elemented too i.e. being a part (of the whole).
more eminent i.e. of greater importance.
As, in the firmament The stars reflect the light from the sun, thus we can see them; just so is love made clear by spring though it comes from 'loves awaken'd root' (in the soul).
spheares i.e. the 'heavenly spheres' which according to ancient astronomical belief, revolved round the earth.

A Nocturnall upon S. Lucies day, Being the shortest day

The day is 13 December, thought to be the shortest day, the winter solstice when the sun goes into the sign of the goat or Capricorn. Lucy (light) was the name of Donne's patroness the Countess of Bedford, and possibly the poem was written at a time when the lady was ill. A superb atmosphere of near death, with the year at its death being used as a symbol, is created, with the poet calling himself the 'Epitaph' on earthly events. The five verses have nine lines each, and in the second the poet anticipates the 'next world' (death) but here named as 'spring'. The idea – like the idea of the phoenix – is that of renewal, of rebirth, either in the after-life or such as spring provides. In the third verse the poet speaks of himself as 'the grave of nothing'; he looks back to their past mutual griefs, and how absence from each other reduced them to 'carcasses'. The fourth verse plays on the word 'nothing', with the essential nothingness before creation compared to the nothing which is the separation – a fine distinction which gives the poem at this stage ingenuity and verbal wit and little immediacy beyond that of an exercise. The final verse returns to the idea of the poet as epitaph for this particular day and what it represents.

flasks Stars.
squibs Flashes (but pale ones).
scarce seaven houres i.e. the period of daylight.
hydroptique Having an uncontrollable thirst. (see note, p.36, on 'spungie hydroptique' in 'Elegie: On his Mistris'.)
the beds-feet The earth (the image of a man dying at the foot of his bed is present too).
their Epitaph i.e. the appointed spokesman of this death.
I am every dead thing i.e. I shall not awaken to a new life.
Alchimie . . . expresse i.e. squeeze out or make an elixir of nothing.
He ruin'd mee This really means that the poet is unhappy in love and has gradually been reduced to nothing as a result. His is now a wholly negative existence.
All others, from all things This is about the process of obtaining sustenance from nature.
the whole world, us two Microcosmic again, they were the whole world in grief.
Chaosses i.e. having no direction or point.
absences . . . carcasses Separated in the flesh, their bodies were dead.
Yea plants, yea stones detest Probably derived from Pliny, who notes sexual affiliations between trees, plants and precious stones.
an ordinary nothing . . . I am None i.e. less than a shadow, for a shadow emanates from something.

The Relique

Three verses of eleven lines each, with the elaborate unravelling of the conceit paralleled by the development of the verses. Firstly, couplets followed by alternate lines rhyming, then the triplet at the end of the verses.

The starting point is the poet looking forward to the opening of his grave some years hence; whoever opens it will find his lover's gift, the coil of hair around his arm. Perhaps he will ponder on this attempt of each to keep their souls temporarily together. Should this occur at a particular time they will be made objects of devotion, a devotion that is owing to Love itself. But the real miracle is not their remains, but the manner of their love; it was of a transcendent spiritual nature, reaching beyond sex to the ecstasy of soul communion.

device i.e. this clever idea.

mis-devotion i.e. because rightly God or Saints should be the object of devotion, whereas these are human lovers.

Mary Magdalen Most commentators note that she is shown with fair ('bright') hair in pictures.

harmlesse i.e. causing no suffering to others, innocent and blameless in our love.

the seales,/Which nature . . . sets free The implication is that love is hindered and confined by conventions, but that these lovers – the poet and his mistress – transcended it.

a miracle shee was Note the exaltation implicit in the phrases.

Satyre: Of Religion

Donne's five satires were written at some time in the 1590s, deriving probably from such Roman satirists as Horace and Juvenal, though it is never easy to identify the Latin author influencing Donne at any particular time. This is Satire 3, written in couplets. Pope, whose own style was fastidious, considered it to be somewhat rough. In fact it conveys superbly, through the rhythms and the pauses, the mood of the poet. There is a mixture of anger and compassion, for he is concerned here with human frailty in relation to religion. Note that he refers to religion as 'our Mistresse', for to the young and older Donne, sensual and spiritual references can define his concerns; 'mistress' is synonymous with his love, his wife, his faith. Note too the use of the rhetorical question, and the advancing of the idea that the pagan's devotion to virtue is as meritorious as the Christian's devotion to God. Regardless of religion man can be redeemed by Christ.

There are references to contemporary events (the mutinous Dutch) and to the constant search to find a way through to the Pacific Ocean. Military imagery is also present, with the idea of fighting for the 'Mistresse' and recognizing and rejecting the devil and his power. The argument prepares for the invocation to 'Seeke true religion', but where? Through the Catholic faith, Protestantism here in England, or the Calvinistic views founded in Geneva? Again the parallels with the pagans and their gods are explored and Donne criticizes the extreme narrow-mindedness of many Protestants. Religion, asserts the poet, is universal. Thus the satire is directed against those who have failed to establish this, be they Christian sects or pagan. In a fine rhetorical passage Donne urges the seeking out of truth, and indeed even at this early stage it is a passage which looks forward to the language power of the sermons. If religious truths are enigmatic or mysterious, we should still seek to discover them. We should transcend tyranny, put our faith in God, and refuse to be led astray by earthly needs at the expense of the soul. Again Donne employs the device of the rhetorical question, but the natural imagery of the hill and streams, the concise use of Biblical and historical analogies, the mixture of the colloquial and the elevated – all characteristic of Donne – are here used with devastating effect.

pitty ... spleene Compassion ... anger.
railing Cursing.
worne i.e. that have been there a long time.
the first blinded age i.e. the age before Christ of pagan thought and argument.
valiant Courageous, but here the meaning is 'strong'.
earths honour was to them i.e. the pagans and their worship of things earthly.
As ... surpasse i.e. the pagans may have got to heaven before us!
blinde i.e. pagan, not knowing the Christian religion.
whose merit i.e. their own disciplined lives and code of morality may have got them to Heaven and earned them Christ's redemption.
mutinous Dutch i.e. the Protestant Dutch still resisting the Spanish (Catholic) oppression in the Low Countries.
North discoveries i.e. the North-west passage (to the Pacific).
Salamanders Lizards thought to be able to survive easily in fire.
Children in th'oven i.e. Shadrach, Meshach, Abednego, whom Nebuchadnezzar consigned to the furnace; they were not burned. (Daniel, i,11–30).
fires of Spaine The reference is to the Spanish Inquisition and the burning of heretics.
limbecks Stills.
for gaine beare Suffer for reward.

and his i.e. God's.

forbidden ... appointed Unholy ... holy.

decrepit wayne Decrepit old age (waning).

Mirreus A derivative of myrrh, used in the making of incense. Mirreus is therefore a personification of the Catholic Church and its attendant ritual.

here i.e. England.

Rome The Catholic Church.

ragges Shreds (of cloth) and rituals or trappings.

statecloth Canopy.

Crantz Donne has in view the 'Schismatiks' of Amsterdam (The Will) and their followers.

brave Loves i.e. showy effects.

Geneva Symbolic of Calvinism, of which it was the birthplace.

humors Tastes or practices.

Graius The Greek Orthodox Church.

vile ambitious bauds Donne is comparing certain preachers with procuresses ('bawds'), female brothel keepers who profit from the activities of the prostitutes they procure for customers.

Godfathers Those who provide spiritual guidance.

Pay valewes Fines, usually imposed upon those who did not accept the marriage arranged for them by their guardians.

Phrygius Symbolizes the Phrygians, an early second-century Christian sect inhabiting Phrygia; extremely ascetic.

Graccus (Usually Gracchus); of the Roman Gracchi, a great noble family; here the representation is of a too tolerant attitude to religion and sex.

Of force must one Only one religion is true, do not be forced to say that there are any others.

To stand inquiring right To inquire and to argue may well be right, but to be apathetic or thoughtless is wrong.

On a huge hill This splendid image of nature to symbolize religion is an anticipation of the method of another great religious writer, John Bunyan (1628–88) in *The Pilgrim's Progress*.

none can worke in that night See John, ix,4 for the origin of this.

now doe i.e. search hard for truth.

The mindes indeavours i.e. by trying hard arrive at (the ultimate truth).

Kings blanck-charters i.e. giving rulers a free hand.

Vicars Those acting on behalf of.

boot thee Be of any profit to you.

Philip ... Gregory ... Harry ... Martin Philip II of Spain; Pope Gregory VII, associated with the tenet of the infallibility of the Pope; Henry VIII, who broke from the Roman Church; Martin Luther, founder of Protestantism.

mere contraries Absolute opposing religious sects.

At the rough streames calme head i.e. the power of God himself, which sheds tranquillity on all around.

So perish Soules i.e. so men are lost who trust man's claim of power from God, rather than God himself.

Song

This has wonderful lyrical control, with the first four lines rhyming alternately, followed by a tripping couplet and then a skilfully wrought triplet in which the varying length of line conveys the musical intonation suggested by the title. Verse one is a list of things which are either impossible to discover or undertake. Verse two sees life as a journey in which the search for woman's constancy is paramount: such an ideal, maintains the poet, is impossible. Verse three elaborates on this by asserting that if a true woman were found she would soon become false. Notice the range of references in the first verse, the insistent hyperbole in the second, and the 'Pilgrimage', here to a non-existent shrine, in the third.

catche a falling starre i.e. an impossibility.
a mandrake A plant having forked roots which shriek when they are pulled up, and supposedly endowed with human attributes.
Mermaides singing They were supposed to be temptresses, hence the sirens' songs.
Ride ten thousand daies and nights Perhaps a reference to Spenser's *Faerie Queene* and the Squire of Dames's wide search for a virtuous woman.
true, and faire Pure and beautiful.
False, ere I come A cynical note on which to end the poem.

Song

Possibly written for his wife Ann when Donne travelled to the Continent in 1611. Sometimes the four short lines, with their exquisite lyrical melancholy, are written as two long lines. The conceit in the first verse is that every parting is a kind of death, but in verse two is the promise of a speedy return to his beloved. The third verse is full of foreboding at the thought of some misfortune separating them, while the fourth is a kind of reprimand to her for wasting time in grieving. The final verse, warning her against prophecy that something will happen to him, reminds her that since each keeps the other alive, they cannot in fact ever be parted.

The balance, the sequence and the economy of the poem are apparent; the language eloquent with feeling and pain and, unlike some of Donne's other verse, profoundly simple and direct.

But come bad chance . . . If we suffer ill-fortune we are apt to indulge ourselves with it and make it worse than it is.

sigh'st my soule away Note again the linking of the spiritual and the physical which builds up in this verse.

If in thine . . . the best of mee If she grieves she is in fact 'wasting' her beloved as well as herself.

divining i.e. prophesying, thinking ahead.

The Sunne Rising

Here Donne, by the very nature of his direct colloquial opening, turns poetic tradition on its head, for the conventional poetic address would pay tribute to the love-giving, life-giving qualities of the sun and perhaps address it with reverence. Donne does neither. The sun is a busybody disturbing lovers, and the first verse indicates the range of people whom he should awaken. The rhythmical movement of that first verse almost conveys the stretching of the body on awakening. A couplet of varying length is sandwiched between two lines which rhyme, while the ninth and tenth line of each verse form a climactic couplet, generally longer. In verse two the microcosmic emphasis is again apparent, with what is now a commonplace of Donne analogy, 'the India's of spice and Myne' and the 'Kings'; the natural wealth and the wealth of state and status are as nothing compared with the completeness of the lover's love. The analogies extend into the third verse, and this is really an elaborate reworking of the theme of The Good-Morrow, 'And makes one little roome, an every where'. The colloquial tone is maintained throughout.

Court-huntsmen, that the King will ride A way of dating this poem; James I was addicted to hunting, so it must have been written after 1603, with the courtiers hoping to gain preferment by being seen in attendance upon the King.

countrey ants i.e. farmers busily havesting their crops.

the'India's of spice and Myne A reference not to India, but to the West Indies and East Indies.

alchimie i.e. superficial or flashy.

the world's ... warming us ... This bed thy center is Note again the microcosmic emphasis so typical of Donne.

To Mr *Rowland Woodward*

Rowland Woodward was with Donne at Lincoln's Inn, and they were to remain close friends. This is a moving and wise poem, with an explicit self-irony. It is written in colloquial triplets, and deals with the poet's own 'chast fallownesse', though he looks back on his past writings. He is arrived at the state where he wishes to put aside vanity, coming to the idea that 'There is no Vertue, but Religion'. We must concentrate on the contemplation of ourselves, not in vanity but in meditation, inwardly preparing for the Day of Judgement. Outward things are as nothing; giving and receiving love is all.

fallownesse Linked with 'chast' this must mean spiritual fertility.
love-song weeds ... Satyrique thornes A slighting reference to his own verses.
Omissions of good i.e. we should not turn our back on good deeds; to do so is as bad as generating ill deeds.
stain'd their first white i.e. sinned.
Vice-covering discretion i.e. concealing wrong-doing.
christall glasse Probably a glass which magnifies the heat when placed in the full glare of the sun, i.e. a magnifying glass of that period.
Blowing our sparkes of vertue A continuation of the sun image above.
straw i.e. things in us which are of no value.
Soules of Simples Convert medicinal herbs into liquid form, the process requiring warmth and stillness for successful completion.
retirednesse i.e. looking into ourselves, meditating.
farmers i.e. we work our 'land' – that is, our own destiny lies in the way we cultivate ourselves, the way of life we follow, our spiritual concerns. The image continues until the end of the poem.

Twicknam Garden

Probably written between 1608 and 1617: for the Countess of Bedford, who was Donne's patroness, lived at Twickenham during that period. Grief-stricken, the poet turns to nature in springtime and is prepared to be comforted, but love undermines his response (since it is an unhappy love). Thus, the garden that could have been a paradise is made into a waste land by his mood. The image of the spider is ingenious, that of the serpent apposite if undistinguished.

In the second verse the poet declares that his mood would be more consonant with that of winter, but he asks to be transformed into a mandrake or a fountain so that he may be part of the garden (and not, therefore, an unhappy lover). In the third verse, through an elaborate conceit, he asserts the purity of his own grief, but bemoans the fact that a woman cannot be judged by what she appears to be. Woman is perverse, and by being so injures the poet, probably because she is now being 'true' to another lover.

Blasted i.e. suffering deeply.
balmes Cures, blessings.
as else Which would otherwise.
spider love, which transubstantiates all i.e. poisons everything that should otherwise yield good.
Manna The heavenly food supplied to the Israelites in the desert — wafers made with honey (Exodus, xvi, 14–35).
the serpent brought i.e. the temptation to indulge his envy.
Benight Overtake with darkness.
christall vyals These were placed in tombs in pagan times as a kind of tribute to the person buried there, since they contained a record of their life.
because her truth kills mee i.e. her loyalty to her other lover.

The Undertaking

A poem written in quatrains, with an internal rhyme in the very first line of the poem. The poet claims that his own particular brand of 'courage' surpasses that of the celebrated heroes of legend whose deeds are so often quoted. He has kept quiet about the fact that he has found the true platonic love which transcends the outward manifestations of sexuality; he will not speak of it, for it will be derided by 'profane' men, i.e. those who believe that love is confined to earthly passion. The last verse beautifully, almost poignantly, balances the first, for he speaks to the reader who, if he discovers what the writer has discovered, will prove his equal in remaining silent. What is outward and physical is conveyed through the imagery of clothes, and throughout the poem there is a shrewd insight into human nature and motivation.

Worthies The famous heroes of the past.
specular stone A particular kind of stone thought to have been used in construction in early times. It was supposed to be transparent.
Such stuffe to worke upon i.e. what they can see.
forget the Hee and Shee i.e. sex.
prophane men Those who lust after the flesh and do not believe in the soul.

A Valediction: forbidding mourning

Izaak Walton (1593–1683) in his *Life of Donne* (1640), says that this poem was written to Ann Donne when the poet went to France in 1611, but this is conjectural. A beautifully constructed, economical poem, written in balanced quatrains and highly sophisticated in terms of reference and range of association.

The first verse deals with the ascending of the soul from the body in 'virtuous men', while the second is an invocation to his mistress to let their parting be silent too, for it would be profaning their love to trumpet it for all and sundry. The third verse is a cosmic analogy, with the poet ranging from earthquakes to equinoxes, the heavenly spheres which do no harm. The fourth verse returns dramatically to earthly love which depends on the presence of the loved one. But in the next two verses the poet establishes that he and his mistress are as one, their souls so commingled that absence only refines the quality of oneness. Verse seven explores the conceit of the compasses, but here, perhaps ironically, there is a sexual as well as a spiritual suggestion in the image, and this conceit consummately expresses the fullness of their love for each other in the final verses. The imagery is typically Donne, and the careful student will explore the compasses image, which is much more than the common symbol of faithfulness despite absence.

teare-floods ... sigh-tempests i.e. the kind of language which would be used by poets to convey grief at parting.
the layetie Laymen, in this case meaning those incapable of experiencing or comprehending a love like that of the poet and his lady.
Moving of th'earth i.e. earthquakes.
trepidation of the spheares In ancient belief, these were the hollow globes that moved round the earth.
sublunary Of the earth, beneath the moon.
soule is sense Senses engender physical love.

Like gold to ayery thinnesse i.e. to gold leaf, or to its quintessence.
stiffe i.e. safe.
compasses i.e. dividers, hence symbolic of the substance of the poem,
  and here ingeniously inverted to give hope rather than division.
obliquely Not in a straight line.
firmness Truth, constancy.

A Valediction: of Weeping

Here three verses of nine lines each; a quatrain followed by a
brief couplet, then a triplet to round off each verse. 'A valedic-
tion' means the taking leave or saying goodbye. The conceit
involving 'coines', 'stampe', 'Mintage' is that the tears wept by the
lover are a direct image of the beloved, and this is the central
play on words extending throughout the first verse at the
thought of separation. The second verse, microcosmic as ever,
has the representation of the world compared to the tears and
their subsequent overflowing. The third verse extends the analogy to the moon and the seas and conjures the loved one to say
little for fear of destroying her lover.

whilst I stay here i.e. before I leave you.
coines A deliberate pun, for she makes the tears and they reflect her,
  like the face on a coin.
Pregnant of thee To be born from you.
emblemes of more There is worse to come (the separation).
thou and I are nothing then i.e. because they are separated.
on a divers shore A foreign land.
can lay i.e. by drawing.
A globe . . . thy teares The favourite Donne microcosmic image.
Moone,/Draw not up seas A reference to the pull of the moon on the
  tides, though here of course distorted to sustain the hyperbole.
Example finde i.e. from her sighs – the hyperbole here being the
  implication of shipwreck in a storm.

The Will

Six verses of nine lines each, couplets with the exception of the
last three lines which are in the form of a gradually unwinding
triplet, giving some force to the last statement. The whole poem
is an exercise in wit, the development of a series of conceits and
hyperboles in which the poet leaves his various attributes in a
cynical way to a number of myths, abstractions, people, faiths,

places. There is wisdom and the rich irony of maturity, but the poem is also biting and, at times, bitter.

Argus The Greek giant who had a hundred eyes. He was used as a spy, particularly on lovers. ('Argus-eyed' means 'jealously watchful'.)

Fame Rumour.

To women i.e. because of his unhappy love affairs and the grief they have caused him. He is, of course, being cynical.

who had twenty more i.e. that number of other lovers.

constancie Trust (in the stars).

truth . . . Court i.e. to those who seek preferment and therefore cannot be trusted.

ingenuity and opennesse Honesty and frankness.

Jesuites Because of their ability to twist arguments.

Buffones Clowns.

Capuchin An order of monks vowed to self-denial in an extreme sense.

Schistmatiks/Of Amsterdam A sect practising extreme Puritanical tenets.

Courtship Here the meaning is courtesy, respect.

gamesters Gamblers.

disparity Not equal to her, not good enough for her.

Schoolemen . . . doubtfulnesse The name 'Schoolmen' was given to the teachers of philosophy and theology who lectured in the ecclesiastical schools attached to some abbeys and cathedrals. To them the poet leaves his 'doubtfulnesse' – the Schoolmen must be used to encountering scepticism.

My sicknesse . . . excesse I give my illness to the doctors or to my own self-indulgence.

physick books i.e. medical books.

Bedlam A madhouse (after the hospital of St Mary of Bethlehem in London).

brazen medals Roman bronze coins.

make disproportion Unsuitable (because he is old).

all your beauties Her physical attractions.

to'annihilate all three Himself and his lover and, presumably, love itself.

Revision questions on John Donne

1 By choosing any two poems, indicate Donne's quality as a lyrical poet.

2 What are the main images employed by Donne in his love poetry? You may confine your answer to any two poems.

3 Examine the verse form of any three poems by Donne.

4 By a close analysis of any two poems, indicate the quality of Donne's intellect and his main interests.

5 In what ways is Donne a sensual poet? You should refer to two or three poems in your answer.

6 'Heterogeneous ideas yoked by violence together.' How far do you think this remark by Dr Johnson on metaphysical poetry applies to the work of John Donne?

7 In what ways do you find Donne's poetry morbid? You should give examples from two or three poems.

8 Write a critical appreciation of any two of Donne's religious sonnets.

9 What are Donne's main concerns in his religious poetry? You should refer to any two poems in your answer.

10 Compare and contrast one of Donne's love poems with one of his religious poems, bringing out differences/similarities in themes, treatment, images, etc.

George Herbert
(1593–1633)

The poet and his work

George Herbert, whose father died when he was only a few years old, was brought up by his mother Magdalen Herbert. He was educated first, at Westminster School, afterwards at Trinity College, Cambridge where he received an MA degree in 1616. Already a Fellow of his College, he was destined to have a distinguished university career, becoming Reader in Rhetoric in 1618, and afterwards Public Orator until 1628 But he was more interested in getting into Court circles and making a figure for himself, in the hope of obtaining worldly preferment. In fact he opted – surprisingly in view of his ambitions, though these soon faded – for 'other worldly' advancement by taking Holy Orders. He was ordained in 1626 and, at his own wish, spent the next four years in seclusion. He obtained the living of Bemerton in 1630, taking up office in September, but he was the incumbent for only three years, dying in 1633 at the early age of forty. All Herbert's poetry, virtually like that great 19th-century poet Gerard Manley Hopkins, was devoted to religious lyric and meditation, and he is one of the finest poets in our language – though, understandably, a little obscured by the greatness of Donne. *The Temple* was published shortly after his death and contains his finest verse.

Poem summaries, textual notes and revision questions
Aaron

Ostensibly about Aaron (see Exodus, xxviii), but really about the symbol of devotion. The first verse describes Aaron's garb and ornaments, the second the poet's abject state by comparison, with his defects and his restlessness. Aaron's every mark is countered by one of the poet's. But he has another personality and manifestation, finding the source of all things in Christ. Finally, because he has been 'tun'd' by Christ he becomes Aaron, ready to receive Aaron's flock. A superbly economical lyric; 5-line verses with alternate lines rhyming, but ending in a couplet.

Holinesse on the head See Exodus for the description of Aaron.
A noise of passions ringing me for dead i.e. discordant music.
So holy in my head Note that this verse is a subtle variation and
  repetition of the first.

Affliction

Eleven verses of six lines each with the now familiar pattern of
alternate lines rhyming before the climaxing couplet. The language changes and thus the changes in the imagery are the
salient features of what is a moving and consummately executed
poem. In the first verse God 'entices' the poet, a word virtually
associated with a kind of spiritual seduction. In this happy and
undemanding state the poet is also fascinated by the ritual and
practices of the Church, and its trappings. By verse three, God is
seen as a King dispensing gifts; in the fourth, 'milk and sweet-
nesses', and the poet is still happy in the joys of Christianity. But
a change comes over him, and (from verse five onwards) he
experiences suffering and sorrow. These increase in intensity,
and the tone about God changes too, as he betrays the poet to a
solitary life. Death images are now present; God becomes a kind
of doctor, but again the poet's suffering increases. He is
'betrayed' into more sickness, and ultimately abandoned. Despite all, the poet begs for divine help that he may love God.

brave Noble.
naturall delights My own happiness and abilities.
furniture . . . household-stuffe The trappings of worship – the altar
  etc.
'tice Entice. Used again, to show that the poet is being won by outward
  things.
a world of mirth Again the emphasis on happiness.
reserved Held.
sudden soul caught at the place i.e. service to God in the church,
  'fiercenesse' perhaps being equated with devotion.
straw'd Strewn.
But with my yeares As I grew older so my sorrows unwound and
  brought me, who had not known it, sadness.
My flesh began i.e. my flesh complained to my soul.
tune my breath i.e. make it (groan) – but note the use of 'tune', a
  harmonious word in itself, thus giving suffering a kind of acceptance.
grief did tell me Because I was able to experience sadness, I knew at
  least that I was alive.
edge Sharpness.

a fence Protection.

The way that takes the town By inclination I liked a sociable life.

lingring book...gown Academic or solitary religious life. 'Gown' has also the hint of the funeral shroud – so here a kind of living death.

Academick praise Praise of his studies (which kept him from finding his deep spiritual needs).

crosse-bias i.e. dividing me against myself and you.

Her household to me He feels that if he were a tree he would be serving properly; at this moment he cannot serve God.

stout Stable, strong.

I will change the service Expressive of the doubt he feels – but he soon returns to the service of God.

clean forgot i.e. by God.

Let me not love thee I'd rather not love you if I can't love you fully, but I ask for your help in this.

The Agonie

Typically Herbert in terms of the verse control and the balanced articulateness of the expression. Simply, three 6-line verses with alternate lines rhyming in the quatrain, and each verse rounded off with a couplet. The two immeasurables for the poet are sin and love; sin is the crucifixion of Christ and selfishness in all things. Love is Christ's blood, which tastes like wine to the poet. It is the opposite of selfishness.

Philosophers...Fathom'd...states...kings Notice how this encompasses all the physical world as distinct from the world of the spirit.

behove i.e. it is necessary.

sound them Measure their extent.

Mount Olivet A reference to Christ's agony in the garden there.

presse and vice Burden and force.

To hunt his cruell food Sin, according to Herbert, is positive and predatory in man.

assay Go and taste.

crosse i.e. the crucifixion. Note the important point in this poem that love and sin can be interchangeable, but different to different men; those who put self before God and those who put God before self.

abroach Tapped (the blood of Christ).

bloud...wine Note the reference to Holy Communion here.

The Collar

The restless, fervent quality of this poem is reflected in the metre in which it is written, the 9–line verses having various line-lengths, questions, exclamations – all contributing to the mood of the poem. The poet rails against his past acceptance of his calling, but the whole tenor of the poem is about that decision in the past and his final submission of the word of God – despite the histrionics of rebellion.

I struck the board i.e. in temper, in rebellion.
lines and life Verse and life as distinct from religion.
in suit i.e. bowing the knee.
a thorn i.e. the crown of thorns, symbol of Christ's suffering.
cordiall fruit i.e. something that will restore me.
wine ... sighs i.e. drunk for pleasure, not for any religious reason.
bayes Bay-leaves: poetic rewards.
on double pleasures i.e. really live now.
cage ... rope of sands All images of constraint.
deaths head i.e. inward fears.
Child! ... My Lord i.e. a return to the arms and bosom – and service – of God.

Death

Six verses of four lines each with a rhyme scheme of *abba* throughout. Death was once repugnant, particularly when one considered the after-effects, for example bones becoming sticks. Death sometimes took youth, but since the blood of Christ has been shed, death has new colour, and at judgement day souls are radiant; therefore we can die as we will, without fear, seeing either the dust or the softness of the soul.

effect Result.
shooting short Not reaching far enough.
fledge souls Children.
extort Take from us, perhaps prayers or suffering.
Much in request Because man who dies goes to Heaven – Paradise.
dooms-day The Day of Judgement.
down i.e. swansdown or eiderdown – soft, dust being the earth to which we return.

Deniall

The denial is that of God, with the failure of the poet's prayers to get through to him. The shape of the verses reflects the anguish, with the final short line after the alternately rhyming ones providing a succinct comment on the poet's deprivation. The analogies with music and nature are once more present, with the idea of mending his rhyme containing the idea within it of mending (i.e. improving) himself so that he becomes worthy of God and will thus be heard.

as was my verse i.e. I could no longer write in praise.
disorder i.e. anxiety; I was not myself any longer.
like a brittle bow Note how swift the images are, as swift as moods and changes.
pleasures ... warres i.e. to self-indulgence, or fighting (but perhaps in the imagination only).
benumme This spelling of 'benumb' gives the word a curiously dead quality.
dust i.e. man, who was made from it.
My heart was in my knee One of Herbert's superb transferences.
Untun'd Favourite musical analogy of Herbert's.
Like a nipt blossome i.e. killed by frost, here the lack of response from God.
mend my ryme i.e. so that I can write in praise of you (but also mend myself so that you will listen to me).

Dialogue

Three verses of eight lines each, with alternate lines rhyming in the first four, followed by couplets in the last. As the title suggests, this is a dialogue between man and his saviour; the last (fourth) verse has an extra line from the poet in which he voices his heartbreak. The first verse is self-condemnatory, but the reasoned answer tells him God wishes him to give up his soul to his service. He gives up what he cannot hold, but God replies that he himself endured all things for man, and it is this argument that moves the poet to feel his own heart is broken. God's argument brooks no answer.

waving Probably 'wavering', or even yielding.
ballance ... poise ... measure i.e. do you have the choice, the power of balancing things.
transferr'd th' accounts i.e. what does man owe God, who gave his Son for man? But the image is a contemporary one.
savour Reasoning, understanding.
Sinne disclaims and I resigne I want no part of what is to happen. I disclaim sin.

feel all smart i.e. God's suffering for man, and particularly at the crucifixion.
Ah! No more The poet now feels his own guilt on account of man and thus makes his final statement.

Discipline

The idea is that God does not need wrath: love will conquer all. Alternate lines rhyme in short-lined quatrains that are lyrical and impassioned in the elevation of love as the great connection between God and man.

a full consent Agreement, harmony.
book The Bible.
remove Go away.
Stonie hearts i.e. even the cold ones will be moved.
a man of warre Almost an inversion of the Cupid myth, but beautifully put.
wrought Worked, moved.
Thou art God Note the brevity yet firmness of utterance, redolent of faith.

Easter-wings

Note the shape of this liturgical poem, first printed vertically in the early editions so that the shape of the wings appears on the page. It is cunningly written to describe the fall and then the rise, the crucifixion and the resurrection, the fall of Adam and the redemption of man, the fall of the sinner, then his reclamation. That is the shape. Briefly the description of man being born in wealth (grace) and falling from it inspires the poet in the first verse to aspire, so that the fall will further his own 'flight' towards heaven. The second verse gives the poem a personal application – through self-suffering like that of man, the poet can advance himself and take flight for heaven. The structure is exquisite.

the fall further the flight i.e. the fall must lead to a rise again – we must accept our suffering and sin and redeem them by serving God.
Let me combine i.e. by sharing Jesus's suffering he will rise again, just as Jesus did.
Affliction Suffering, like the suffering of Christ.

The Flower

Seven verses of seven lines each, a common form in Herbert, with the shorter-lined couplet providing a lyrical effect. The rewards of God are as sweet and clean as the flowers in spring, and the poet's heart, shrivelled in the winter, recovers its own greenness. Flowers stay underground during the winter, and God brings about death and an ascent to heaven, and only His word is permanent. The poet longs to be rid of change, to be set in an unchanging paradise; but while he is living on earth he must endure the wrath of God. Yet he regards writing as another form of rebirth, another spring in age. Thus men are like flowers who suffer change, and will be forced to give up Paradise because of their pride.

returns i.e. the goodness that comes from God when least expected.
demean Behaviour, demeanour.
my shrivel'd heart Compare this with Donne's 'Love's Growth'.
blown i.e. lost their blossom.
chiming of a passing-bell i.e. for death, yet signifying immortal life. Note the familiar music image.
amisse i.e. gone wrong.
word ... spell God's word is permanent.
Offring at heav'n Trying to get to Paradise.
straight line i.e. on earth, upright man.
relish versing Enjoy writing poetry.
tempests fell all night i.e. tossing and turning with worry.
Swelling Becoming self-important.

The Forerunners

Six verses of six lines each, alternate lines rhyming followed by a climaxing couplet. Age is catching up with the poet, and he feels himself being reduced because he is not as sharp as he was, though he still has God. As long as he can still please God by his writing, he must have some happiness. He says farewell to his past language, which had its own enticing and sinful qualities. The penultimate verse works towards the idea that 'Beautie and beauteous words should go together.' If he is old now, let his language be still lively in praise of God. Again the skilful elaboration of the conceit is quite apparent.

harbingers Those sent ahead of a royal procession to arrange lodgings for the retinue.

dispark i.e. lesson my abilities and ideas.

they left me i.e. his fears.

best room Heart.

passe not Don't care.

dittie ... fine and wittie Note the sudden flippancy of tone, almost an introduction to his past self and the language he then used.

knew the doores i.e. the outside.

Brought you to Church Wrote about religion.

sugar-cane Note the excessive, cloying sweetness.

bane Ruin, curse.

stie ... broider'd coat ... him that sings i.e. will you ruin yourself despite your beauty and also hurt your begetter, the poet?

dung i.e. rubbish.

canvas ... arras With a coarse covering, not a richly wrought tapestry.

Beautie and beauteous words Note the reduction of what he is saying to this perfectly balanced sentence.

passe not See note above.

bleak palenesse i.e. the oneset of age – though life is rich within and the mind is still active.

Jordan

Strongly satirical poem in which the baptismal power of Jordan is implicitly contrasted with the springs of pagan inspiration. Three 5-line verses with alternate lines. The attack is on the conventions of poetry, of false verse; the poet's own emphasis would be on inner truth, not on superficial things. Analogies are drawn with stairs and furniture as manifestations of outwardness; the language of poetry and its obscurity is condemned. Let others do what they will, the poet can simply praise God.

fictions Imaginary things.

lines i.e. the way things are made, whether they be stairs or poems.

enchanted groves i.e. the language of conventional poems.

coarse-spunne Ill-constructed.

vail'd Obscure, hidden.

at two removes i.e. at the second attempt (to understand).

pull for Prime Go straight to the real meaning.

Jordan (II)

Almost a reminiscence of his coming to write poetry in praise of God, and how that poetry was carefully dressed and artificial. Nothing was too good for God, so he wrote and re-wrote. But he felt that 'a friend' (i.e. God) might call it mere pretence, and that love itself is already itself expressed and only needs copying to be felt. Three 6-line verses, with alternate lines rhyming.

my lines My verse.
quaint words ... trim invention i.e. unusual expressions, neatly turned.
as if it were to sell As indeed it is selling the praise of God to God and any who would listen.
if I were not sped If I hadn't finished.
quick ... dead Note the excellent antithesis, the opposites in fact reflecting his past verse and his present.
the sunne i.e. God.
joyes ... trample on his head i.e. the joys of heaven.
wide Empty.
readie penn'd Love in itself is the complete expression.

Life

A beautiful poem, with flowers as a symbol of life. Three 6-line verses having two couplets each, with the flowers symbolic of death as well as life, since they wither and die but leave their scent with the poet. In their death he gets the foretaste of his own. If his life is like theirs, however, his purity and innocence and brevity may approximate to theirs. There is some mysticism here, but the essential thing is that goodness and beauty in flower and in soul are to be sought.

my remnant What remains to me.
did steal away i.e. died, or their souls left them as they died.
Times gentle admonition This reprimand or warning from time (about his own time).
sugring Sugaring (sweetening) the thought of death, which is the immortality of the soul, or union with God.
cures Remedies. (Also, flowers are planted around graves, thus 'curing' loss.)
I follow straight I will join you immediately.

Love

Three 6-line verses, with alternate lines rhyming and the climaxing couplet at the end of each verse. This beautiful poem is a fitting end to the selection here. Love is God, and so bounteous is his love that the poor sinner can enter Heaven. God identifies the sinner, but accepts the sin and takes the self-acknowledging repentant man into heaven. Christ has borne the blame for man's sins, and man will serve, thus tasting 'the meat' of love in the perfection of God.

dust Contamination.
slack Holding back.
my deare Note the colloquial tone, marking the approachability of God.
Who made the eyes but I? God made everything.
marr'd them Spoiled them (by looking on things I shouldn't have watched).
who bore the blame? i.e. Christ.
taste my meat i.e. share my love, kingdom, goodness, heaven – once again Herbert has chosen the simple analogy of food for the complicated symbol of goodness from God.

Man

The invocation is to God by way of talking of Man, and the second verse indicates the range of what man is. He has speech and reason, everything in him is in harmony and is related to everything else. Everything on earth is for man, and so is everything in the heavens. Everything descends to man from God. The seas are for man, and he possesses the earth completely. The microcosmic focus is more marked towards the end of the poem where the poet says that man is himself a world 'and hath/Another to attend him'. (Compare this with Donne.) The concluding verse states that God made man in his perfection, and that man must therefore serve him in return for the service of the world which is his. The verses are of six lines each with a varying length of line and a complex and irregular rhyme scheme.

stately habitatior ... therein The idea is that God lives in man.
to whose An economical way of saying 'compared to whose'.
They go upon the score i.e. their speech is derived from ours.

symmetrie Perfectly proportioned.

And all to all the world i.e. he was made in relation to the world and its particular functions.

amitie Friendship, harmony.

moons and tides The comparison is one of relationships, for the tides are dependent on the moon just as the feet are on the head (brain).

got so farre Developed so completely.

dismount Can see.

He is in little all the sphere He is the microcosm of everything. (Note the modern spelling of 'sphere' here.)

their acquaintance Their likeness.

cabinet Private room.

descent* and *being . . . ascent* and *cause i.e. from God, coming down to earth or rising to heaven.

dutie Function, i.e. are useful to us.

Waters united . . . all things neat The most difficult section of the poem. Briefly: we have the seas to navigate, and when they divide we are on land; on land they provide drink, as rain they are food; they wash us. Their element is perfect – like the whole, of which they are one element.

Man is one world A further extension of the microcosmic emphasis.

a Palace i.e. man.

wit Intelligence.

Mortification

A meditation on the shortness of the life of man: six 6-line stanzas with a varied length of line and an *abc abc* rhyme scheme. The bed is equated with the grave in youth, and at the same period music is also a knell to the grave. There is an unequivocal morbidity about the first three verses; in maturity the house that encloses the living body is a symbol of the coffin that will enclose the dead one. In age the chair or litter is an emblem of how he will be conveyed to 'the house of death'. The final verse is an invocation to God to 'instruct us so to die,/That all these dyings may be life in death'. There is a certain obscurity in this elliptical construction at the end, but the idea is that man lives in death as in life.

chest of sweets Perfumed chest.

clouts . . . winding sheets i.e. the birth clothes are the grave clothes – he is playing upon the similarity, though in a sense life is death since we are born into sin. (And of course infant mortality rates were much higher at that time.)

who are bound for i.e. those who die young through fever or some sudden illness.
the knell The music of the church bell 'tolling' somebody's death.
Schooling Disciplining, i.e. not allowing them to roam and rove.
inclosure i.e. the house.
Marking Noting.
thawing i.e. getting tremulous and tearful.
biere Bier: the platform or stand on which the corpse or coffin is placed before burial.
a solemnitie i.e. a funeral scene.

The Pearl

Six verses of ten lines each with alternate lines rhyming, and a central rhyming couplet. The poet ranges over the areas of knowledge he has acquired, but always returns to the love of God, which is above all other things. In the second verse he contemplates the ways of the world and its deceits, and this re-affirms his love of God. Next he considers the various pleasures of the senses, and again asserts his love of God; the final verse places the responsibility for his love of God on the ways of God himself.

head ... pipes ... presse i.e. whence special knowledge comes.
huswife, spunne As a good housewife, at her spinning wheel, has spun.
starres conspire What fate decrees.
forc'd by fire i.e. what is revealed by fire (for example, smelting etc.).
stock and surplus What we know and what we we've got more of.
vies of Competing for.
moldeth it Moulds it (to react or behave in a certain way).
true-love-knot He is being ironic – these are the outward manifestations of love.
bear the bundle i.e. carry out the ways of the world (in order to get preferment or find favour).
propositions of hot bloud and brains i.e. passions and enthusiasms.
unbridled store i.e. self-indulgence.
flesh, not brasse Feelings, not metal (or money) – but ironically twisted from the Biblical 'all flesh is grass'.
one to five i.e. one body to the five senses – hearing, sight, taste etc.
sealed ... eyes The sewing up of the hawk's eyes so that it will be untempted by other prey.
main sale ... commodities Note the continuation of the commercial imagery from verse one.
labyrinths i.e. the tortuous paths (or mazes) of the world.

groveling wit i.e. getting what I can (a self-critical term).
Silk twist Fine image to suggest a silken ladder leading man to God.

Prayer

A conventional sonnet, which reads like a devotional exercise – at least in the octave, where the various associations are used, with almost a ransacking of related imagery. Prayer is the food of the Church, God's breath in man, the expression of the soul in man, of the emotional pilgrimage of faith, a thunderbolt against God, the spear entering the side of Christ, the miracle of the six-day creation – these indicate part of the range. But the sestet is rich in personal expression, there is a poignant change of mood and we feel that we are hearing the sincere prayer of a man of faith, for although the range continues with a run of Biblical references, the balanced simplicity of the ending compensates for the extremes. Prayer is simply 'something understood'.

Angels age i.e. as old as the angels are.
plummet A lead plumb used by anglers to determine the depth of water (but here used figuratively).
Engine Thunderbolt.
transposing Here the meaning is 'making, creating'.
Manna Spiritual food.
Heaven in ordinarie i.e. God is everywhere, in commonplace things.
The milkie way The stars.
the bird of Paradise . . . the land of spices i.e. things of beauty.
something understood i.e. dependent on the intellect, a rational appraisal of prayer.

The Pulley

Four 5-line verses, with the idea of a beneficent God in the first verse giving man all his blessings except rest; if God had given this final blessing, then man would have worshipped all the gifts instead of God. Thus man will be restless, never having everything, and this weariness may bring him back to the bosom of God.

Contract into a span Be reduced into this very small area.
stay Pause.
the bottome i.e. of the figurative 'glasse of blessings'.

rest Find comfort in.
repining Discontented.

Redemption

This superb parable is in the form of a sonnet. The reference is purely contemporary, the tenant having a Lord and making suggestions to him. But the effect is profoundly spiritual, the Lord being equated with Christ; consequently what is said has a running duality and innuendo about it. The second part of the octave establishes the Lord as being in heaven but he is, so to speak, an absentee landlord, since he has business on earth.

The 'tenant' returns, seeks the Lord among important people but finds him with thieves and murderers. He is at Calvary – this is the Crucifixion – and Christ grants him his suit: in fact he dies for the tenant and all others with suits. The beauty of the poem lies in its economy, its control, the masterly organization of the sonnet to suit the message or allegory the poet wishes to sustain. The couplet, like the couplet of the courtly love sonneteers, provides the perfect climax; the difference is that it holds (as Wordsworth was to put it some two centuries later) 'thoughts that do often lie too deep for tears'.

rich Lord God.
suit Request.
small-rented lease i.e. a reduction of his rent, here meaning a reduction of his dedication to God.
Long since on earth i.e. the sending of Christ to redeem mankind.
cities, theatres ... courts Notice the fine contemporary effects, which would bring home the message of the poem even more clearly.
theeves and murderers i.e. those with whom Christ was crucified.
Your suit is granted i.e. take what you will (for I will redeem you).

The Temper

A direct invocation to God, and a moving admission of weakness. The verses are quatrains with alternate lines rhyming. The poet prays to be allowed to rest with God, but if he must first be tortured, this will make him all the fitter to accept later happiness. God is able to 'Make one place ev'ry where' – an echo of Donne's famous line in rather a different context. The balance of verses is superb, the economy of utterance expressive of simple anguish and unquenchable faith.

The Temper The title refers to the tempering of the soul by God through adversity, as steel is tempered by fire.

thy love in steel i.e. strongly, with great power.

my soul ... My soul Note that the repetition has a kind of hymnal quality.

tent ... grave Note the play on space, hence on the vastness of God and the smallness of man.

Wilt thou Note the doubt implicit in the question.

thy way i.e. to cause me suffering, to test me and thus to make me worthy of you.

tuning ... Musik An exquisite way of making suffering harmonious and even beautiful.

Vanitie

A remarkable poem, rather similar in range to *Agonie* but with a somewhat different shape, and the full idea worked out in each verse. Four 7-line verses with alternate lines rhyming, short lines balancing the longer ones. The astronomer knows the heavens and what they portend, the diver gets pearls from the seas to his own danger and that of his mistress. Then the chemist can analyse all he finds in man and make him ready for life too. The moral of the last verse is that by searching at various levels for what brings about death, the searchers fail to find the life that, richly endowed by God, is all about us. This is a very carefully constructed poem, each verse being a complete entity in itself, with the twist in the final verse. God is everywhere but man misses him because he misses out on life.

fleet Quick, sharp.

bore Penetrate.

stations i.e. their positions in the heavens.

their dances Movements.

full-ey'd aspects ... secret glances i.e. what they reveal (portend) and their secrets.

with his side i.e. the moment and impetus of diving.

ventrous Venturing, adventurous, reckless.

Her own destruction Because it represents vanity, and is therefore destructive of the soul.

his danger i.e. the risks he takes in the sea, and the risk of having a mistress who advertises herself to others by the wearing of pearls.

subtil Chymik Clever chemist.
devest Divest, take off (clothing).
They appeare trim and drest i.e. he has helped them to prepare to face the world (perhaps by cosmetics etc.).
Embosomes i.e. embodies.
To finde out *death* A fine last line; man finds *death* by mistaking the mechanism of the world for the maker; this is his vanity.

Vertue

The masterpiece of Herbert's poetic output. Four verses in lyrical mode with alternate lines rhyming, the line at the end of each verse having a moving finality. Through the contemplation of nature in small and great, the poet traces the cycle of life and death that is the lot of everything except the soul, which can survive all changes including death. The poem's impact is immediate and moving – it conveys a profound truth.

bridall i.e. the marriage or wedding-feast of earth and sky.
angrie i.e. because red, flushed.
rash gazer i.e. one who looks and is thus moved to tears by the beauty he sees.
grave i.e. the earth.
sweets Sweet smells, scents.
My musick . . . closes It rises and falls; Herbert's favourite music analogy applied again.
Like season'd timber Wood that has stood the test of time (just as man is tested by God).
turn to coal i.e. is burned up.
chiefly lives Because the virtuous soul is immortal.

Revision questions on George Herbert

1 Write an essay in appreciation of any *one* poem by Herbert that makes considerable use of analogies from nature.

2 In what ways is Herbert an intellectual poet? You should refer to two or three poems in your answer.

3 Write an appreciation of any two poems by Herbert which you would describe as *lyrical*.

4 What is the distinguishing quality of Herbert's faith as expressed in his poetry? You should refer to as many poems as possible in your answer.

5 What do you find specifically metaphysical in Herbert's verse?

6 In what ways is Herbert's poetry dramatic? Refer to two or three poems in your answer.

7 Consider the economy and structure of any two of Herbert's poems, bringing out their individual qualities.

8 In what ways is Herbert a major poet, worthy to rank with Donne? You should refer to a range of poems in your answer.

Richard Lovelace
(1618–1656/7)

The poet and his work

John Aubrey (1626–97), author of *Brief Lives*, gives an account of Lovelace that reveals a personable, essentially attractive man – rather different in calibre and attitudes from Suckling and Rochester, surviving Suckling's era and hardly living into Rochester's. A Kentish gentleman and the son of one, Lovelace was educated at Charterhouse and Oxford. He was particularly attractive to women but was of a modest deportment and refined nature, as far as we can gather. In 1642 he presented a petition to the House of Commons for the restoration of the King's rights. Because of this he was imprisoned, but went abroad for about three years in the mid 1640s, returning again to a period of imprisonment. The King was executed in 1649, and Lovelace was later released, though his latter years are thought to have been spent in quiet retirement. According to Aubrey he was in considerably straitened circumstances for the last part of his life.

Poem summaries, textual notes and revision questions
To *Althea*, from Prison

This was written in 1642, when Lovelace was imprisoned after presenting the petition to free the King. Four 8-line verses with a sureness of touch. Alternate lines rhyme, each verse having a symmetrical balance. There is a certain courage inherent in the poem, and the general effect is richly imaginative. Imprisoned, the poet's imagination is still free to be with his mistress (note the juxtaposition of 'fetterd' in line six of the first verse). The second verse compares the greater freedom of wine drinkers with the limited freedom of fish in the sea. The third verse is an outspoken and courageous assertion of loyalty to the King. The final verse, with its immortal opening lines, stresses the freedom in love and the freedom of the soul, insisting that only angels enjoy a like liberty. The bravery of the poem is matched by the simple bravery of the language – what begins as a conceit in the first two verses takes on a seriousness of tone and a timeless nobility of utterance in the last. It is one of the finest lyrics in our language precisely because it unassumingly but honestly sets freedom of conscience above the physical freedom we all crave.

Gates The prison bars.
tangled ... fetterd Note the images of imprisonment; a clever ironic working-in of his state.
wanton Sport about.
Cups Drinks.
allaying Restraining.
Loyall Flames i.e. passionate love.
committed Linnets i.e. committed to song.
should be i.e. because at the time of writing (1642) he had been usurped.
Inlarged Winds Gales.
Hermitage i.e. a retreat.

To *Amarantha*, That she would dishevell her haire

This delightful poem has some seven verses of four lines each, each verse consisting of two rhyming couplets. The focus is on the beauty of a woman's hair when it is unconfined. The conventional poetic imagery is employed, but with again a fine balance and economy ('But shake your head and scatter day'); but although the lovers make love, the language is largely unsensual because of the conventional conceits mentioned above. The last verse bemoans the passing of time, which changes the nature of such beautiful experiences.

shining haire The brightness image is to be perpetuated throughout the poem.
Ravisher A looking forward to their love-making.
spicie Nest i.e. her sweet-smelling hair.
confest Admitted to be.
ravelled Here the meaning is 'wound up' (not unwound).
o're-cloud Blot out (by binding up).
scatter day i.e. shed light everywhere from your tresses.
See 'tis broke Once her hair is dishevelled, once it is in its natural state, this is the signal and the start of their *natural* love-making.
Creame ... milke-baths i.e. they will make love in complete nakedness.
Wells ... i.e. when they have drained each other dry.
our very sorrows weepe i.e. regret that things change, that we cannot love like this forever.

The Grasse-hopper. To My Noble Friend, Mr *Charles Cotton*

A beautiful poem written in longer quatrains, with alternate lines rhyming, beginning with an invocation to the grasshopper in the wheatfields; the joys of the open-air life are continued until the frosts, when the grasshopper becomes the creature of the hearth. The second half of the poem brings in Charles Cotton, and the focus is on the depth of their friendship and shared study and experience. It is a poem of two reflecting halves, the second's conclusion drawing on the moral of verse five.

haire Stalk.
Oaten Beard i.e. wheat.
Delicious teare The dew.
reard i.e. whence you came (God created everything).
Poppy i.e. when sleep takes you.
gilt-plats Golden plates.
Sickle Of time and the harvest.
Ceres and ***Bacchus*** Goddess of Plenty (Harvest) and the God of the vine (drink).
verdant i.e. green (perhaps also 'inexperienced' here).
Peirch (Probably perch).
o're flowing glasse i.e. rain on the windows.
Vestall flames From the 'Vestals', virgin priestesses dedicated to keeping the flame of the Roman goddess Vesta always burning.
Ætna The famous volcano, very active at times, in eastern Sicily.
in Epitome Symbolizing the volcano.
Hesper The evening star.
Tapers Lights, candles.
That wants himselfe i.e. he who is lacking (in mental or spiritual resources) is worthless.

Gratiana dauncing and singing

This is exactly what it suggests, a poem of description and observation. The usual poetic devices are employed, nature and also using classical associations and parallels. Each of the four verses has a couplet at the beginning, and the six lines end with an *aab ccb* rhyme in each verse. This is still a lyric, but with a somewhat stronger rhythm – as befits the subject – in each of the verses. Note that a differently named mistress is the recipient of each poem, perhaps indicating that these are merely courtly exercises on related themes.

as the Sunne Note the commonplace imagery.

Law and poyze i.e. rule and balance.

a Starre i.e. Gratiana.

Firmament i.e. the idea is that the pavement has become a sky itself.

Atlas The Titan in Greek mythology compelled to support the sky on his shoulders for his rebellion against Zeus.

all the Deities i.e. gods and goddesses.

pav'd with broken hearts i.e. because of the beauty of her movements and of herself.

Harmonious spheres i.e. the 'music of the spheres', heavenly or celestial music.

Graces . . . Apollo The second the God of the lyre and hence of music; the first the three sisters in Greek mythology who were the givers of charm and beauty.

To *Lucasta*, Going to the Warres

Perhaps the finest of Lovelace's lyrics: noble, economical, balanced, in an antithetical flowing measure which has three verses with alternate lines rhyming. The result is an aesthetic and imaginative experience, poignant in its moral insistence, yet quiet and unassuming in the essentials of its expression. There is an easy yet masterly play on words throughout, with linked images producing the aesthetic effect referred to above. Simply put, the poet is going to war, and leaving his mistress. The tone is as pure in its simple faith and duty as his attitude towards his mistress. The balance is exquisite, inverted word-order giving the final line the stamp of firmness and immortality.

Nunnerie . . . chaste breast Note the immediate linking of the images.

and Armes Herewith the word-play – he is also flying from the arms of his mistress.

a new Mistresse . . . chase The idea is immediately picked up from the preceding verse.

Foe . . . Field . . . Faith Note the alliteration that contributes to the musical effect.

imbrace Again note the play on the word, which has physical and mental connotations.

Inconstancy It merits personification, in view of the seriousness here instead of the conventional use of the term.

(Deare) Again, a measure of the fine balance – the same as (Sweet) in brackets in the first verse. The form of the poem is almost like a circle in terms of its emphasis.

Honour The call of duty.

The Scrutinie

The conceit or wit of this poem is that the poet has been loyal to his mistress for some twelve hours; this is a tedious length of time. He must have others to love, just as she must, though he may ultimately return to her when he tires of other loves. Though the tone is cynical it lacks bitterness, and is a realistic appraisal of a way of life that at least puts a premium, in the poet's eyes, on honesty, and self-honesty first. Four verses of five lines each, alternate lines rhyming, but with a couplet at the end of each verse.

forsworn/Since thine i.e. already promised to you.
That fond impossibility i.e. that I would be true.
all other Beauties wrong i.e. because I should give them none of my love.
black and faire Gold and coal, blonde and black-haired beauties, a superb double meaning.
Mineralists Experts searching for ore.
loved my round i.e. gone around, making love to other women.
pleasant Almost a derogatory word – the most 'pleasing' of the lot.
spoyles i.e. having accomplished the seductions of others.
Varietie Having enjoyed a number.

Revision questions on Richard Lovelace

1 Write an appreciation of two of Lovelace's lyrical poems, bringing out clearly their main qualities.

2 In what ways is Lovelace different from Rochester and Suckling? You should quote from the three poets in support of your answer.

3 Do you find Lovelace a sympathetic poet? Give reasons for your answer.

Andrew Marvell
(1621–1678)

The poet and his work

Andrew Marvell was born in 1621 in Yorkshire; three years later his father, a clergyman, removed with his family to Hull, which was nearby. Marvell as a boy attended Hull Grammar School. He wrote Greek and Latin verse in his teens, and in 1633 he went up to Trinity College, Cambridge. In 1638 his mother died, his father remarrying some six months later. In 1639 Marvell obtained his BA, but returned to Cambridge until 1641, the year of his father's death. While at Cambridge, Marvell had a brief flirtation with Catholicism.

He spent much of the 1640s travelling abroad, and one or two of his occasional poems were published. But 1650, when he was twenty-nine, witnessed his first marked poetic utterance, 'An Horatian Ode upon Cromwel's Return from Ireland'; shortly after this he became tutor to the daughter of General Fairfax. It seems likely that Marvell remained at Appleton House, the Yorkshire home of the Fairfaxes, until some time in 1652; then in 1653, on the recommendation of Milton, he very nearly achieved a State appointment. The same year finds him in Eton, where he lived in the house of Oxenbridge, who twice visited the Bermudas, a subject for one of Marvell's poems written at this time.

In 1656 he travelled on the Continent again, as tutor to young William Dutton, and in 1657 came his State appointment, that of Latin Secretary at the salary of £200. With Cromwell's death in the following year Marvell produced a poem on the Lord Protector, and early in 1659 he became Member of Parliament for Hull, which town he was to represent for some twenty years. He continued to travel on the Continent, staying at embassies, and wrote the occasional satire and epigram, the sixties being a busy time for him. *The Rehearsal Transpos'd* was published in 1671, the second part in the following year, and in 1674 he brought out his poem inscribed to the second edition of *Paradise Lost*, in which he says of Milton:

Thou sing'st with so much gravity and ease,
And above human flight dost soar aloft.

Marvell's last years were given over largely to attacks on
Catholicism, and in 1681, three years after his death, his miscel-
laneous poems were issued. He lived well into and survived the
change of the Restoration period, and he remains perhaps the
most sophisticated and elegant of the metaphysical poets. Compared with Donne his verse is smooth, but like Donne, he is
— epigrammatic; Marvell's conceits and wit are refined where
Donne's are hewn in the rock of faith or leap with the indulgence of sensuality. Marvell, like Donne, transforms the conventional (for example the pastoral), into an ironically individual
and stimulating exercise. Like Donne's poetry Marvell's is
steeped in mathematics, science, and theology; also in contemporary relevance. Donne's skill is in variety of paradox, word-
play, the whole enlargement of the mind both in life and in
death; Marvell's skill is in the delicacy with which he describes
nature or the soul in nature. He is recognizably the poetic heir of
Donne, and recognizably his own man too.

Poem summaries, textual notes and revision questions
Bermudas

Written some time after 1653, for Marvell lodged at the time in
the house belonging to John Oxenbridge, a Puritan who had
suffered at the hands of Archbishop Laud some twenty years
earlier, and who had in fact paid two visits to the Bermudas.
There is a superb rhythmic effect, as of the waves against the √
boat or even the movement of the oars, and the whole has the
effect of a psalm, its musical current, so to speak, being the
major part of its charm and pathos. The couplets are flowing
rather than end-stopped, thus keeping time with the movement
as well as contributing to it. After the sufferings and endurance
of the voyage, there is a fine consonance between the lush and
fertile descriptions, approximating to a fertility of faith that
transcends what has happened and what is to come. The poem
conveys an intensity of a spiritual fervour.

Bermudas A group of islands in the West Atlantic, taking their name
from the Spanish navigator and historian Juan de Bermudez, though
the islands were discovered before his own visit in 1515.

And yet far kinder A direct reference to the persecution of the Puritans mentioned in the summary above.

Sea-Monsters This is thought to be a reference to a fight between the natives and two whales in *The Battle of the Summer Islands* by Edmund Waller (1606–87).

Prelat's Bishop's.

enamells Embellishes, makes smooth.

Ormus Or Ormuz. Ancient city on the Persian Gulf.

Apples Pineapples.

Ambergris From the sperm whale.

He cast . . . Gospels Pearl The image suggests the casting of pearls before swine, and therefore by association this is an ironic usage, for the jewel they have discovered is the freedom to enjoy and promote their faith in God.

the *Mexique Bay* The Bay of Mexico; the arm of the Atlantic bordered by the United States, Mexico and Cuba.

The Coronet

Moving religious poem, with an individual style though couched basically in the pastoral mode. A mixture of alternate lines rhyming and couplets, with a controlled varying length of line; the expression is contrived, as fits the convention, with flowers and garlands symbolic of an attempt to redress the crown of thorns won by Christ. This is thus a redemption poem, with the temptation imagery of the Garden of Eden very much present. Service to God is to replace human love, but of course the poet is tempted from this by thoughts of personal ambition. The invocation is to God to cause the serpent – the devil – in man to wither, just as the flowers and garlands must die too. The last line is an exquisite balancing again of opposites.

Thorns i.e. the crown of thorns worn by Christ (Matthew, xxvii,29).

Towers Very high 'towering' headdresses worn by women and fashionable at this time.

Shepherdesses The conventional way of addressing one's mistress in the pastoral tradition.

Chaplet A small wreath of flowers, worn on the head – corresponding to and contrasting with Christ's crown of thorns (above).

wreaths i.e. coils (of the serpent, the tempter).

debase i.e. lower the value of the 'diadem' – the real, heavenly crown.

Snare i.e. trap.

curious frame The reference here is to the chaplet, which is elaborately wrought or constructed.

both their spoils i.e. on the serpent and on the flowers.
May crown thy Feet The conceit indicates that God treads on the
  crown (the chaplet made in that form) and the head or crown of the
  serpent.

The Definition of Love

The poet defines his love in terms of the metaphysical imagery
he loves to employ, so that the poem (whose theme is the
romantic one of 'star-crossed lovers'), has a scientific and
mathematical exactitude, and the precise 'definition' is consonant with the form. The result is a series of quatrains which have
both a cosmic and a microcosmic significance. It contains much wit,
the elaboration of conceits, antithesis and a running personification and idiomatic control, all of which make it stimulating to
read. If it is a 'definition' it is a personal one, and it is a logical
teasing of the mind. In other words, it is an intellectually
challenging poem based on an intellectual conception.

for object i.e. the loved one.
Magnanimous Despair Note the heavy personification and, here, the
  peculiar quality of Marvell's use of oxymoron in this phrase which is
  followed by the epigrammatic terseness of 'feeble Hope'.
my extended Soul is fixt To where my soul/love is directed.
Iron wedges i.e. comes solidly between (apparently from Horace's
  Carmina I, 35,17–18).
her Tyrannick pow'r If the lovers came together they would be
  triumphing over Fate, which has decreed that they may not.
the distant Poles i.e. they are completely separated.
Convulsion Earthquake.
a *Planisphere* A chart, the projection onto a plane.
Lines . . .*oblique*. . .*Paralel* As the poet says parallel lines never meet.
  The concept is a geometrical one.
Conjunction Uniting or meeting.
Opposition of the Stars They are indeed 'Star-crossed lovers'.

A Dialogue between The Resolved Soul, and Created Pleasure

This poem, probably dated prior to 1645, is as its title indicates
in the form of a dialogue between the soul and the senses, with
comments and interventions from the Chorus. For the most part
the verse is in couplet form, though there is an effective use of
the variant quatrain from time to time. The expression is

mannered, balanced, sophisticated. Briefly, the soul is resolved
to resist the lure of the senses; the imagery used to describe the
soul's preparation for this resistance is the figurative language of
battle. Pleasure personified urges that the soul – 'Heavens Heir'
– should put aside battle and prepare instead to indulge the
senses, enjoying rest and perfumes, for example. The soul
resists these blandishments, and has rational answers, cleverly
turned, for each temptation offered. The sense of sight, and
hence of vanity, is then used by Pleasure, but the soul prefers the
'Heavens ... we cannot see'. The soul is tempted by the hearing
of music but continues to resist, and the Chorus, in true Greek
tragedy manner, comment on the brave sight this resistance
provides. The Faustus-like temptation continues, but the soul
triumphs, for to seek out the truth of things one needs the
humility that the lure of the senses lacks. The poem is therefore
a moral fable, the dialogue a mode of exploring the lures of the
senses as distinct from the independence of the mind, the spirit
or the faith.

Helmet ... Sword. ...... Army Note that the images are 'Christian
 soldier' images such as those used by Bunyan in his hymns and in *The
 Pilgrim's Progress*. See also Ephesians vi,16–17.
Divine Immortal.
Nature wants an Art Nature lacks cunning.
heighten i.e. add to, enhance.
I sup above i.e. in heaven, on insubstantial, unearthly things.
bait Pause for refreshment.
thy Side should strain i.e. lest you should be made uncomfortable, a
 very ironic overtone from the poet.
Is Heaven's and its own perfume An example of Marvell's economy
 and the picking up of one phrase quickly and giving it a finely
 different turn.
Crystal Mirror.
the posting Winds recall A subtle inversion – a reminder of the winds,
 so light are the musical sounds.
Chordage i.e. the music is compared to chains or bonds, hence this is a
 pun on chord and cord.
fence/The Batteries Hold off the assaults.
Charges Calls to attack.
fair, and soft, and sweet Note the simplicity, therefore the directness
 of the temptation.
Beauty The temptations are of the flesh.

A Dialogue between the Soul and Body

This contrasts deliberately, one suspects, with the *Dialogue between the Resolved Soul and Created Pleasure*. There are three verses of ten lines and one of fourteen, a curious lack of shape, therefore, for a Marvell poem. There is much word-play, many connected images, some of a paradoxical nature, and the debate is economically, almost elliptically constructed. The argument, for such it is, is between the soul and the body, the body resenting what it considers to be the soul's tyranny. It compares the soul to a fever. In a superb final sequence the body compares the actions of the soul upon the body to the work of architects who take trees from the forest for building. Throughout this final sequence there is a heavy personification of abstractions.

Dungeon The body.

bolts ... fetter'd ... manacled Note the prison imagery paradoxically employed on what has no physical substance, the soul.

blinded ... drumming Note the vivid sense effects, almost like those of a surrealist painting.

Chains ... Tortur'd Continuing the prison image.

double Heart i.e. the valves, but the theme of dissonance or deception is being sounded.

stretcht upright i.e. its permanence and integrity, making the body straight.

mine own Precipice I go I fall down because of this (the above).

needless Not wanting (the soul).

anothers Grief i.e. the body's sufferings.

Diseases ... Cure A focus on the maladies the body suffers. The Cure is 'worse' because until the body dies the soul is not released.

Hope ... Fear ... Love ... Hatred All these are emotions, feelings that the Soul makes the body experience, and which the body considers worse than physical illnesses.

foregoe Forgo, do without.

have the wit i.e. the innate knowledge of me to be able to make me suffer in this way.

Eyes and Tears

Finely controlled octosyllabic couplets set in a fluent and economical verse-pattern of four lines each verse complete in itself. The conceit starts with eyes, which see and also weep, the tears being a true index to what has been seen. The poet turns to his own tears and and elaborates by comparing tears of happiness and laughter. He has been moved by the beauty of nature, just as the sun is moved and produces showers, the cosmic tears. Tears are blessed; there follows an analogy with Mary Magdalene and her tears that bathed the feet of Christ. Further elaborations on the conceit include references to the full moon, pregnancy, a return from a journey, desire moved to compassion; and a beautiful image calls the stars 'Tears of Light'. It is a beautiful and sustained lyric, its main, moving message being that seeing is weeping.

complain Weep.
Self-deluding sight i.e. gets the wrong perspective.
Poise Balance (following the Scales image).
Pendants Connected with 'Jewels' in the line above, a good example of Marvell's work and the building up of connected sequences.
the Red . . . The colours of the flowers, but with religious associations as well.
No Hony, but i.e. the only honey was the tears (at the sight of so much beauty).
Chymick i.e. practises alchemy.
Essence i.e. what is distilled, the quintessence.
***Magdalen* . . . liquid Chaines . . . fetter** Note again the strength of the religious element *and* the fact that another sequence of connected images is here enhancing the pathos of the concept.
full sailes Ships with a large cargo.
***Cynthia* Teeming** The full moon.
Drench'd i.e. (desire) is washed out by tears.
double Sluice Double because there are two eyes to weep.

The Fair Singer

This is a conventional courtly poem, the compliment being turned on the lady's beauty and singing. Three 6-line verses have alternate lines rhyming in the quatrain and a climaxing couplet. As usual the balance of the poem is exquisite. There is much personification throughout. The lady's eyes captivate the poet's heart, but her singing makes inroads into his mind. Again the imagery of 'fetters' is used to convey his enslavement to her, and later the fighting imagery too is used to show the completeness of the lady's triumph.

both Beauties i.e. Love and the sweet Enemy.
subtile Cunning, subtle.

Forces i.e. my advantages.
gained both the Wind and Sun i.e. got into the most strategic position.

The Garden

Again this poem would appear to have been written during Marvell's stay with Fairfax as tutor to his daughter. There are nine verses of eight lines each in the now familiar octosyllabic couplets. This is a poem in celebration of solitude, meditation and the appreciation of nature and tranquillity. It contains many of Marvell's most memorable lines. There are puns and highly idiosyncratic and epigrammatic usages, as well as fine sound- and colour-effects and a consummate use of antithesis. The classical analogy is always to hand, and the effect is one of art and artistry in form and expression. Not a word is falsely placed, not an emphasis that is not consonant with the mood. The rhythm of the poem is itself indicative of peace and the achievement of that inner harmony which is at once rare and rewarding.

vainly i.e. in vain.
amaze Bewilder.
Palm ... Oak ... Bayes Rewards for victory in war, governing in peace, and poetry.
some single Herb i.e. one tree or herb supplies each of the rewards mentioned above.
their Toyles upbraid i.e. discreetly criticizes their labours (but note the half-pun on Toyles which is like the coils of hair 'up-braided' into plaits).
close i.e. join.
Your sacred Plants i.e. those plants associated with the abstractions Quiet and Innocence.
rude i.e. loud, uncouth.
white nor red i.e. the colour of lips and cheeks.
am'rous Loving.
Fond Attentive.
Flame Passion.
run our Passions heat Used up our sexual energy.
retreat i.e. from the 'busy world of men'.
Apollo ... Daphne ... Pan ... Syrinx Apollo, Greek god of medicine, archery and music, whose plant was the laurel, pursued Daphne, who was changed into a bay-tree (*Laurus nobilis*). Pan, Greek God of flocks and shepherds, pursued Syrinx, a nymph who was changed into a reed in order to escape him. He invented the musical pipe of seven reeds and named it after her.

curious Fine.

Into my hands Note that the action is transferred from the poet to the inanimate fruit, thus enhancing the quality of the experience.

The Mind, that Ocean Natural growth on land is balanced by the growth in the ocean.

streight i.e. straight away, at once.

Annihilating i.e. cutting everything down to.

a green Thought ... Shade One of Marvell's most quoted lines. The repetition has the effect of a fresh thought and the fresh shade which accompanies it at the same time. Thus man and nature are in harmony.

vest i.e. the vesture, the outer covering.

whets Attends to, preens.

for longer flight i.e. to immortality through death.

Help ... meet Note the pun – helpmeet: companion; and what assistance could be more suitable.

To live in Paradise alone Without 'helpmeet' (or the serpent!).

Dial i.e. the garden, through its flowers, is itself an indicator to the seasons.

milder Made less (because of the flowers that act as a screen).

Zodiack The sweet-smelling flowers.

Computes Works out or allots.

An *Horatian* Ode upon *Cromwel's* Return from *Ireland*

Cromwell returned in May 1650 and then proceeded to prepare for the invasion of Scotland in July of the same year. Marvell would be obliquely involved here, since his employer General Fairfax resigned rather than be involved in the attack, and Cromwell took over as general commanding the Parliamentary troops. The poem is finely shaped, as one would expect, but perhaps the most stimulating aspect for any reader is what appears to be a deliberate ambiguity, a sharp edge of irony, for the poet's sympathy appears to lie one way according to one reading and the other way depending on the emphasis. The main literary influences would appear to be certain Odes of Horace (as one would expect from the title), and of a translation of Lucan's *Pharsalia* by Tom May. This translation would certainly have been known to Marvell. Marvell's fine sense of balance is here seen in the form of the poem, with its couplets in pairs enhancing each other and together forming a complete statement. Another interesting fact is that the 1681 edition of Marvell's poems lacked this poem except in one copy.

forward Youth Ambitious writer.

Muses **dear** The subjects most dear to his verse.

languishing i.e. in a low key, or perhaps even the 'languish' of love poetry.

Corslet A piece of armour for the upper part of the body.

inglorious Not leading to military achievement.

thorough his own Side A vivid picture of Cromwell in conflict with some of his fellow Parliamentarians.

Emulous One who admires, and imitates the admired person.

And with such to inclose . . . It is better to join (a man like Cromwell) than to oppose him.

Caesars **head** That of Charles I, executed in 1649.

Laurels i.e. the laurel tree (here the crown) which is supposedly immune to lightning, just as the King was thought to be immune by Divine Right (but wasn't).

Bergamot A very good type of pear.

the antient Rights The kingship and its loyalties.

emptiness . . . penetration i.e. vacuum is bad, but over-occupation must give way so that there is room for one only – here obviously Cromwell.

Hampton Hampton Court.

Caresbrooks **narrow case** Carisbrooke Castle on the Isle of Wight, to which Charles escaped, and where he was betrayed by the governor.

Royal Actor . . . Tragick Scaffold Note the ironic tone and the very deliberate choice of imagery.

bloody hands An indication that the poet's sympathies here lie with the King.

He . . . **Scene** Note the italics, and hence an underlining of the comment above. These two lines are again among the most quoted of Marvell's today.

helpless Right The Divine Right of kings, now powerless.

assur'd the forced Pow'r Ensured the triumph of the Cromwellians.

A bleeding Head . . . the Architects . . . In digging up the ruins of a temple the diggers found a man's head which was intact; it was thought to be symbolic of the future power of Rome, according to Pliny.

in one Year tam'd August 1649–May 1650.

both act and know Yet again one detects some irony in this phrase.

sway Influence, hold power.

Commons Feet The House of Commons.

A *Kingdome* Ireland.

forbears i.e. does not push or trumpet (his own achievements).

ungirt Taken off, removed.

sure Safely, for certain.

presume Achieve.

Caesar . . . Hannibal The invaders and conquerors of France (Gaul) and Italy.

Clymacterick The fatal point, the utmost threat.
Pict The Scots, a reference to the forthcoming invasion.
Valour sad True (but misguided) bravery.
the Plad Plaid.
mistake Doesn't find him.
in near On the track of.
the force it has i.e. the power to keep off evil spirits.
A pow'r must it maintain If force is used and triumphs, it will have to
  be used again, an ominous appraisal of the truth of things, and a little
  cynical about what Cromwell has actually achieved.

The Mower to the Glo-Worms

A four-stanza lyric with alternate lines rhyming, this poem flows
through the apostrophizing of the glow-worms. The first verse
has the association with the nightingale; in the second the essential sense of perspective; the third the glow-worms' practical use
to the mowers in the darkness; while the fourth has a delightful
twist in which the poet says that his mistress has so distracted
him that their lights could not show him home anyway.

matchless Songs does meditate The idea is of the bird rehearsing –
  perhaps silently – what ultimately emerges as something of 'matchless'
  beauty.
portend Foretell. The idea is that real comets do foretell evil.
presage Indicate the future (of the grass).
officious Performing a function (to light the way).
foolish Fires Will-o'-the-wisps.
wast Waste.
displac'd Disordered.

The Nymph complaining for the death of her Faun

Deaths of pets often provided material for poetry in classical and
pastoral tradition. This was probably written during the period
1650–1652, and it is in the flowing octosyllabic couplets which
are seen at their finest in 'To His Coy Mistress'. There is a
curiously menacing note in the reference to the 'wanton
troopers', with the idea of irresponsibility linked to that of perhaps serious interference, and the heroine's tone is also a little
suspect. There is also religious content to the poem. The
heroine's grief is naïve, and her faith tells her that beasts must be
treated as people in terms of justice. She broods on the guilt, and

by a natural transition moves to her treatment at the hands of her lover, Sylvio (a common choice of name in pastoral convention) who gave her the faun — which now symbolizes in its death the death of their love. The simplicity of the verse matches the simplicity of the heroine, who tells of feeding the faun, her races with it, and of its feeding on lilies and roses; so it epitomizes the innocence not only of the girl but of faith too. The death-agony is given a strong spiritual overtone, but the idea of preserving the tears shows Marvell adding pagan associations to the strongly Christian ones present in this poem. The final conceit has the heroine seeing herself carved as a statue, with the faun in alabaster at her feet.

Troopers The Scots Covenanters, who fought on the side of the Puritans early in the Civil War.

Deodands Anything that caused the death of a human could be forfeited.

which doth part Is separated from.

Heart Note the pun (hart) repeated later in 'dear'.

counterfeit False in his love.

beguil'd Subject to his influence.

grew wild Either passionate or inconstant.

Smart Wound, suffering.

game Gambling.

it seem'd to bless The faun becomes a symbol of goodness and innocence; the religious tone varies in intensity and direct reference.

fleet Quick, fast.

pretty skipping Note the onomatopoeic effect, and indeed a running alliteration throughout the poem.

Hindes Deer.

it should lye Where it might be.

Lillies Also symbols of purity.

pure virgin Perhaps like the heroine, but with associations with the Virgin Mary.

holy Frankincense One of the gifts of the three Kings who travelled to see the new born Christ.

brotherless *Heliades* The first of the pagan references, here to Phaethon's sisters turned into poplar trees. Their tears became amber.

Vial . . . crystal Tears A common practice in ancient times.

Diana's Shrine Diana was the goddess of the hunt and the symbol of chastity.

Turtles Turtle-doves, of a beauty and innocence matching the faun's.

Elizium In Greek mythology, the dwelling place of the blessed after death.

Ermins The stoat, which has a white winter coat.

bespeak Ask to share.
Let it be weeping too A reminiscence of Niobe, who is represented as a
statue weeping for her children.
bemoane Grieve for.
wear Become part of.
White as I can i.e. pure, but not white as in 'pale as death'.

On a Drop of Dew

Probably written during Marvell's stay at Nun Appleton House
as tutor to General Fairfax's daughter Mary in 1650–51. There
is a Latin counterpart to this poem. Here is a cleverly constructed poem which has both lyrical and contemplative facets, the
alternate lines rhyming and varied by couplets and running
rhymes picked up in the exquisitely shaped verse paragraphs.
The contemplation of the drop of dew, an entirety in itself, gives
way to an analogy with the soul. The soul, complete within itself,
is a reflection of heaven just as the drop of dew was a reflection
of the physical heaven which has let it fall. The final analogy, in
finely balanced couplets, is with the manna gathered by the Jews
(Exodus xvi). Thus, as so often in Marvell and in metaphysical
poetry generally, the starting point (the drop) leads to expansion
of the conceit (the soul), thus indicating a unity in all things from
the smallest to the greatest.

Orient Having the lustre of a pearl.
Mansion Home (in the rose).
For Because.
Globes Extent i.e. in its shape it mirrors the great globe of the sky
whence it came.
Like its own Tear An exquisite image which enhances the running
personification of the subject.
divided from the Sphear Separated from heaven.
Trembling lest it grow impure Become soiled. This really points
towards the contemplation of the soul, which has a like fear.
Fountain of Eternal Day i.e. immortality.
The greater Heaven in an Heaven less i.e. it reflects heaven in itself, a
microcosmic focus by Marvell.
coy Here the meaning is 'modest and unassuming'.
the World excluding round The word which surrounds it.
girt Made ready.
Manna's sacred Dew The food, honey-based, which the Jews were fed
in the wilderness through a miracle.
White, and intire, though congeal'd and chill. A sensitive linking of

the soul and the drop of dew, in a balanced line.
th'Almighty Sun i.e. for the dewdrop, but for the soul, God.

The Picture of little *T.C.* in a Prospect of Flowers

The now familiar pastoral setting and treatment, the subject perhaps Theophila Cornewall whose sister of the same name had died shortly after birth. Five 8-line verses with a regular rhyme-scheme, the last two lines being a couplet with the shorter line first. The prospect is the mental view of the subject, but a physical view too, with the poet seeing the child playing on the grass and naming the flowers. The second verse contains a forward look at what she may do to the hearts of men in later life; this being so, the poet wishes to see her as she is now. The next verse embodies the conceit that she may be able to endow the flowers with more of their own qualities; while the fifth urges her to gather flowers not buds, since they, like she, must further our hopes by a later blossoming. There is a somewhat morbid note about this last verse.

golden daies Childhood, happy life.
Aspect Looks, appearance.
chaster Laws Innocence.
Bow ... Ensigns Cupid's bow, his emblems or attendants.
compound Sign a treaty with.
parly Parley; discuss terms for making peace.
force to wound Their strong ability to injure (by making someone fall in love with them).
that yield i.e. those who give in (they treat with contempt).
the errours i.e. the faults (in nature, in spring).
procure i.e. bring about.
Flora The Roman goddess of nature, the countryside.
make th'Example Yours i.e. that you too may die 'in the bud'.

To his Coy Mistress

The most completely successful, in terms of ironically working out a conceit, of all Marvell's poems, and with the usual finely chiselled fluency in the verse, each word employed with wit, and an exquisite sense of perspective. Time is precious, and the invitation is that they should enjoy it while they can. But it is an exercise, elevated into poetry by the proportions and the tone, which is sustainedly mocking throughout – though with over-tones of sensuality, not to say lust.

coyness Modesty, but false modesty is implied.
long Loves Day A (centuries-long) day given over to making love.
Indian Ganges The great river of Northern India sacred to the Hindus.
Humber i.e. the Humber estuary on which Hull stands.
the Flood The Deluge described in Gensis vii and viii.
vegetable Finely ironic word here, meaning capable of growth and perhaps reproduction but of course without intelligence or sensuality.
you deserve Again note the ironic tone of the address.
lower rate i.e. less than (you deserve). Again ironic.
winged Charriot A famous image, expressing movement – and the violent changes effected by time.
quaint Honour Another shrewd appraisal of her misguided idea of chastity.
But none I think do there embrace. A good piece of metaphysical wit.
with instant Fires i.e. of passion.
let us sport us Note the sensual rhythm of this, and the sudden physical movement of the verse corresponding to the physical act of love.
slow-chapt i.e. the jaws gradually devouring.
Iron gates some editions, **grates** i.e. either the gates of death or the taking of her virginity savagely. But certainly 'iron' is associated with grates.
yet we will make him run Generate passion.

Revision questions on Andrew Marvell

1 Write a close analysis of any two poems by Marvell which make use of the pastoral convention.

2 Write a critical appreciation of either 'The Garden', 'To His Coy Mistress' or 'The Definition of Love'.

3 Which form do you think suits Marvell best? You should refer to two or three poems in your answer.

4 Write an essay on Marvell's ability as a lyric poet.

5 In what ways is Marvell a religious poet? You should refer to two or three poems in your answer.

6 Indicate, by close reference and quotation, the metaphysical qualities to be found in Marvell's verse.

John Wilmot, Earl of Rochester (1647–1680)

The poet and his work

Rochester was born in 1647. His father died when he was ten years old: Rochester went up to Wadham College, Oxford, and received his MA in 1661 after a year's residence. After this he went on the then customary tour of the Continent, then returned to London, where his wit and personal attractiveness commended him to the Court of the restored Charles II. There was an artistic and cultivated atmosphere about the Court, as well as the licentiousness and vice that have so often been described. Rochester abducted an heiress, Miss Malet, and was apprehended and placed in the Tower. He served with the Navy at Bergen, returned to marry the heiress, acquired the reputation of a rake, but made some responsible speeches in the House of Lords. He wrote lampoons and libels, and in 1673 was banished for writing a satire against the King. The real joke is that Rochester supposedly handed the offensive description to the King in the belief that it was something else.

Rochester then set up as a quack doctor under the name of Alexander Bendo, writing his own descriptive brochure to accompany his new career. But in 1677 his early excesses caught up with him; his health began to deteriorate, and he retired and began to repent the viciousness of his life. At the end he recanted all his licentious poems, and died at the age of thirty-two. As a gentleman he could hardly publish his poems, and in any case, many that were not his, but were sensational, were attributed to him. His poems were first collected in 1691. Rochester's is a consummate art, brief, fertile, ironic, succinct and lyrical.

Poem summaries, textual notes and revision questions
Love and Life

This is the high-water mark of Rochester's achievement. The three 5-line verses are filled with lyrical and ironic intention, yet there is a serious undertone; the backward look at the past is nominally without regret; the practical look at the present is insistent with the commonplace of the period: let us love while we can. There is a superficially cynical third verse to round everything off. The short poem is so balanced, so carefully wrought, that it would appear to cover a lack of purpose that does provide a genuine regret, though it is unvoiced in this poem. It appears to be a lyric with a pathetic and moving corollary: that life for the writer is ending anyway.

giv'n o're Over and done with.
Phyllis The irony implicit here is that Phyllis could stand for anyone, perhaps the more anonymous the better.
by Miracle But in view of the religious associations of the word, one is aware of a keen insight into human nature and an understanding of the deprivation of not having a settled life.

The Mistress

A good example of Rochester's method, with constant personification and a perfect balance maintained in the flowing and harmonious quatrains. The first verse looks at the past and how short that seems, while the second examines the effect of absence from the beloved, and how short periods can seem interminably long. Here Soul and Love are equated in an elliptical construction. The conceit is elaborated in the third verse, so that absence now becomes a tomb, though, paradoxically, a living one. This paradox is turned into hope, for 'Short Ages live in Graves.' The next verse considers how his beloved's eyes drive him to distraction; the following tells others not to misunderstand and censure the supposed disagreement between him and his beloved. There then comes a cunning inversion of conventional attitudes and feelings, for the fact that the lovers feel jealous shows that they love 'to an Extream'. Imagination weaves falsehoods, but jealousy, doubt and fear are the real basis of love. One is left with the feeling that this is a witty, tongue-in-cheek poem, which cynically reverses accepted views. But it is by no means merely clever; there is feeling behind the façade of the verses, and intuitive insight into the human heart in the whole conception.

Age ... Day Note how the poem relies on antithetical balance like this one.
Life and Light i.e. the beloved.

shade Shadow, spirit.

On Shades of Souls and Heav'n knows what Note the attack on 'soul' poetry and the contempt expressed by the throw-away words in the second part of the line.

profoundly dull Another knock at the poets who cannot write from experience, since they lack the ability to feel.

Sacred Jealousie ... Proof A paradox, since it is the reverse of what is generally said and believed.

Fantastick Fancies fondly Note the alliterative emphasis that here personifies the abstractions some other poets write about.

fixt i.e. firm, unshakeable.

A Song

The first verse, in the familiar quatrains – here in all four verses – mocks the conventional languishing attitude of the lover away from his mistress. He asks to go, so that his mind may experience what it is like to suffer; then, after this, he will return to his Love, completely contented to die in her arms. He fears that if he should stray again after returning to her, he will lose his own chance of happiness and tranquillity. The language is very simple, the lyrical quality sure and deftly balanced, the whole a pretty exercise in ironic acceptance rather than of cynical wit.

The straying Fool i.e. the lover who cannot do anything but mourn the absence of his mistress.

Fantastick mind My poetic imagination (a mockery of those who live by verse alone).

base heart unblest i.e. someone with whom I might have an affair.

my Everlasting rest i.e. because of guilt, and also because he now has lost his claim to her.

A Song of a Young Lady. To Her Ancient Lover

Three verses in couplets which rhyme but have six lines in the first verse, eight in the second and twelve in the third. A refrain line occurs at the end of every verse, a line which embodies the love of the girl for the old man. Again this is the reverse of conventional love, so that there is again an ironic and mocking quality. But, and this is where the poem scores, it has a moving and pathetic quality too, expressive of the wishes of the old to be young and virile again and to be beloved by someone young; there is therefore an element of wish-fulfilment in the poem which gives it a poignant content. It is, also, sexual in the Donne, Marvell, and Carew tradition, but with a peculiar individual turn that is unusual in a young poet. Perhaps, however, we should remember that Rochester had by then had a lifetime of experience.

flattering Youth i.e. young lovers who importune me.
Aking, shaking Note the internal rhyme, the alliteration, and the fine brevity.
Brooding i.e. deep with passion.
a second Spring The beginning of the sexual imagery.
Nobler parts i.e. sexual organs. An ironic phrase.
Ice i.e. impotence.
Vigor stand i.e. the erection of the male sexual organ.
Art ... without Art i.e. my skill as a lover and, on the other hand, 'art' in the sense of artlessness, without premeditation.

Upon Nothing

A conceit elaborated through a succession of triplets, with a witty paradox, of course, inherent in the conception. From nothing was created everything, and so the wit develops through a subtly catalogued account of how things actually came to be. The 'Great Negative' is balanced by '*Something*', but the poem takes in a range of contemporary references and is basically satirical in tone and purpose, with everything not only beginning but also ending in nothing.

Shade Death, spirit or shadow.
well fixt Permanent.
boundless Wide-stretching.
fruitful emptiness's Note the effect, ironically and satirically, of this paradox.
Matter ... Form ... Light All these constitute Something, the offspring of Nothing.
Body, thy Foe i.e. because of its substance it is the Enemy of Nothing.
destroys their short-lived Reign i.e. by death, the body is made into nothing.
Womb i.e. of nothing, which is what everything is reduced to.
Laick The laymen, the ordinary mortals.
the Wise i.e. all philosophers' views in fact amount to Nothing. The burden of the poem becomes increasingly satirical.
the vast designs i.e. political moves and strategies.
least unsafe i.e. because they are not in conflict with those who oppose

them, and are thus less insecure of office.

With Persons highly thought A verbal shaft at the politicians and people of high rank but little ability in the state.

Lawn Sleeves . . . All these are marks of status in State, Church and the Law.

French **Truth . . .** ***Danes*** **Wit** The poet is mocking a supposed quality in each nation by indicating the lack of it – that there is Nothing of that quality there.

The great Man's gratitude . . . All promises in fact amount to nothing; gratitude soon evaporates: a profoundly cynical view of human nature.

Revision questions on the Earl of Rochester

1 Write an appreciation of Rochester as a writer of lyrical verse.

2 In what ways is Rochester an unusual poet? You should refer to two or three poems in your answer.

3 What are the main poetic devices to be found in Rochester's poems? You should quote in support of your answer.

Sir John Suckling
(1609–1642)

The poet and his work

Greatly popular before the Puritan Revolution and, after his death, in the Restoration period, Suckling was born a gentleman and, like Rochester, proceeded to demonstrate that such a state of privilege could easily be abused. He was a gambler, particularly at cards and bowling, and was constantly in debt. Aubrey gives us most information about him. After attending Trinity College, Cambridge and Gray's Inn, he spent some time on the Continent, the fashionable way of passing one's young manhood at the time. He even engaged in foreign service with Gustavus Adolphus, but in the period before the onset of revolt he was at Court, where his extravagance continued. He had a play produced in 1638. Shortly after the Civil War had begun he became involved in a plot and, fearing that he would be arrested, went to France, where he later died (or, as Aubrey puts it, committed suicide). Suckling is the master of the exquisite short lyric; in the words of a later, greater poet, Alexander Pope, Suckling had the art of saying 'What oft was thought, but ne'er so well expressed'. He is the archetypal Cavalier lyricist, smooth and musical, but, like Rochester, with a keen insight into the human heart and the conventions that it demands and conceals.

Poem summaries, textual notes and revision questions
Song ('Out upon it . . .')

Four verses, quatrains with the second and fourth lines rhyming in each verse. The conceit is that inconstancy is of the nature of man, and that constancy for a short period of time is the only possible measure. It is a frank admission of sexuality, without any softening screen of convention or pretence. The result is an engaging lyric which carries one along with its own wit and verve.

Out upon it A colloquial; phrase meaning 'Let's admit it.'
fair weather If things continue as they are.
Time shall moult away his wings i.e. change (as man does). An original and apposite figure of speech.

agen Again.
a constant Lover Punning on the word 'constant'; irony at his own
  expense.
made no staies Remained.
Had it any been but she If it had been any other woman but this
  beloved (of the past three days!).
A dozen dozen in her place i.e. I would have loved any number of
  others.

Song ('Why so pale . . .')

Probably the best known of Suckling's poems, with its fine control and the refrain line artfully varied. Why be sad if you can't
move your mistress, is the theme of the first verse, while the
second puts a like comment on the negative effects of silence.
The third verse, in brisker rhythm, is quite unequivocal – if
nothing will move her she is worth nothing – let her go to the
Devil. There is a cynical man-about-town tone to the poem, but
the bald summary given here does scant justice to its musical
quality and assurance. The poem is a mockery of the conventional forms of wooing and being sad as a result, and one gets
the impression that for Suckling the grass (to employ the old
cliché) was always greener on the other side of the hill.

Prithee . I pray you.
Will . . . pale Note the varying alliteration in the verse which provides
  much of the music.
Sinner Note the subtle change, a cynical underlining of the ironic tone.
win her . . . doo't The ease of control allows Suckling the double rhyme
  and the conveniently colloquial one.
take her . . . take her Again note the word-play, the idea of taking her
  fancy, influencing her (or even taking her sexually) contrasted with
  the idea that she is not worth taking anyway, and the Devil can have
  her.

Sonnet ('Of thee kind boy . . .')

Strictly this is not a sonnet, but a poem or song, in three deftly
controlled verses. The actual form, with a cleverly varied length
of line, is two rhyming couplets followed by a quatrain in each
verse. The initial invocation is to Cupid, the god of love, but it is
an inverted invocation. For the poet is not asking for anything
outstanding in his beloved, just the opportunity to make love to

her. The second verse develops this by arguing that there is no such thing as beauty; (in the words of the cliché, beauty is in the eye of the beholder). The third verse extends the analogy and, like other writers, Suckling finds a convenient point of reference in the appetite for food and sex. The analogy with the watch being wound up as an equivalent to sexual excitement again shows Suckling's debt to the metaphysicals and, more particularly, to Donne.

(kind boy) Cupid.

know-not-whats i.e. patches ('beauty spots'), commonly used on their faces by society women as an enhancement of their beauty. Suckling is mocking the practice.

mad enough i.e. with passion.

love in love The act of loving itself.

cosenage i.e. being 'conned' or misled.

Lik'd certain colours mingled We may have liked one thing, but that does not stop us from liking something different now.

The fancy doth it beauty make i.e. beauty is in the eye of the beholder.

'tis the appetite i.e. for sexual love.

A Pheasant is i.e. a beautiful bird and hence, by analogy, a woman I desire.

What in our watches ... found i.e. we are like our watches, with a mechanism that can be wound up.

height and nick ... No matter by what hand or trick i.e. we are brought to sexual pleasure by no matter what woman or device.

Sonnet ('Oh! for some honest...')

As with the previous poem, this is hardly a sonnet. There are five verses, this time of seven lines each, with three rhyming couplets in each verse and an unrhymed last line that sometimes produces a throw-away effect, at others a climactic one. In the first verse the poet longs to know whether dead lovers wear chaplets (wreaths) if they were scorned in love, or if used kindly in love on earth. His own feeling is that those who have enjoyed love will be found crowned in heaven, for it would be torture to die and see your mistress in someone else's arms. In justice lovers should lie with their true loves after death; perhaps those martyred by love will have some reward in heaven. But the poet concludes that he would rather have the mistress here and now — yet another 'let us love while we can' poem, though with rather a different early and middle section from others of the genre.

unbodied post Spirit.

shades World below, death.

nobler Chaplets i.e. wreaths binding the brow (perhaps nobler is a pun
 – nobler lovers, or nobler wreaths).

to the being i.e. to be.

have our Loves enjoy'd i.e. loved while we could.

posture State.

agen Again.

Elizium Elysium; paradise after death.

Sophonisba Married to Syphax, King of Numidia, but captured by
 Masinissa, her betrothed, who finally caused her to take poison.

his who lov'd her Masinissa.

Philoclea In Sidney's *Arcadia* she loved Pirocles, and was beloved by
 Amphialus.

Bayes The laurel crown of the poet.

Revision questions on Sir John Suckling

1 Write an appreciation of the two Suckling songs here,
bringing out the individual quality of each.

2 Write a critical analysis of Suckling's two sonnets, saying in
what way they are typical metaphysical poems and in what ways
they differ from the genre.

Henry Vaughan
(1621/2–1695)

The poet and his work

Henry Vaughan was born in Brecknockshire, his family being
distinguished in the area though somewhat run down because of
the irresponsibility of the father. Vaughan and his twin brother
spoke Welsh as their first language, but the conditioning
influence on the poet was undoubtedly the terrain he was born
into – valleys and hills. Vaughan entered Jesus College, Oxford
in 1638, but decided to go to London to study law in 1640. He
was there during the period of the outbreak of the Civil War in
1640, though little is known of his activities until he returned to
Wales, this time to practise medicine in 1647. He married, and
was certainly a Royalist during the troubles, in which two of his
friends were killed, and his brother deprived of his living as a
clergyman. *Silex Scintillans* (1650), translated as *Sparks from the
Flint*, contains some of Vaughan's best verse, and in 1678 he
published a series of 'pastimes and diversions'. He lived
peacefully as a country doctor, and died in 1695; he is buried in
Llansaintfraed. He was greatly influenced by another fine metaphysical poet, George Herbert, who, like Vaughan, was a
strongly devotional religious poet.

Poem summaries, textual notes and revision questions
Cock-crowing

Eight verses of six lines each, the first four in each verse with
alternate lines rhyming, the last two lines of each a rhyming
couplet. The first verse expresses the idea of God's 'Sunnie seed'
endowing the bird with his particular qualities. The birds wait
for the dawn, seeming to be divinely intuitive and responsive,
unlike man who appears not to respond to the breath of God.
The fourth verse begins the direct invocation to the seed of heat
and light germinated in man by God; man even takes his rest
within the divine ambience of God. If birds are given the power
of God's seed, then surely man must respond with his, which has
conferred on him the immortal soul. The final verses are an

appeal for God to break 'this Veyle' so that man may aspire to Heaven, to God himself.

Father of lights Epistle of James i,17.
tinn'd Held.
tincture A slight tinge, small amount.
impowre Engender, give.
thy own image i.e. man, who was made in the image of God.
thy appearing hour The dawn itself, when God appears as the sun or light.
meer blast Wind.
It never opens i.e. it lives in ignorance of salvation.
Ægyptian border The darkness on the land of Egypt in Exodus x,21–3.
earnest throws Throbs of sincerity.
this Veyle Indicates, when removed, dedication to the Lord God. (2 Corinthians iii,13–15.)
gleams and fractions spies i.e. only able to see fragments and reflections (of the goodness of God).
Lilie The symbol of light.

'Come, come what doe I here?'

This poem was almost certainly occasioned by the death of Vaughan's brother William in 1648. Three verses of nine lines each, with a mixture of alternate lines rhyming and rhyming couplets. There is an exquisite but mournful lyrical note that has, inevitably, an elegiac turn. The lament is brooding, but the power of God is always present. The poet's strong longing to be with his dead brother is evident.

each houre, one Again note the fine economy.
Cut off Reduce.
Dayes are my fears Another fine economy.
soiles Smears, besmirches.
No house of store Typical of Vaughan – an idiosyncratic usage meaning where souls are kept, perhaps ready for the day of Resurrection.
To wake in thee i.e. in death, with God, he will not be divided from his brother.

The Dawning

The dawning is that of the Judgement Day, and much of the

poem is devoted to speculation as to when exactly that will be. The Bridegroom is Christ in Vaughan's figurative expression, with the second coming of Christ to judge man as the motivation of the poem. For the most part, the poem is divided by a careful variation in the length of line but, throughout, it is in the form of the rhyming couplet – invocatory, exclamatory, ecstatic and at times melancholy.

The Bridegroome's Comming See Matthew, xxv for the reference to the wise and foolish virgins and the phrase 'you know not the day nor the hour'.

run Occur.

mad man without measure A vivid phrase expressive of immoderation and evil. This kind of reference is part of Vaughan's strength – he is the creator of powerful pictures rooted in the imagination.

descry Show.

the only time Note that the poem is in praise of Dawn, and that Dawn symbolizes the true light of judgement.

chime Harmonize.

hymns i.e. the singing of the birds, the waking of nature.

shadow i.e. of God.

pursie Distended.

in the Van At the head of the procession.

puddle Symbolic of corruption because stagnant, dirty.

securitie Complacency.

vocall *Spring* Superb phrase to convey the 'stream' of feeling and the meaningful power of nature. It is also the stream of faith.

Commerce . . . dust i.e. be subject to the sins of the flesh.

the Sun A common pun on God and Christ and the Sun which gives life and strength.

drest Ready for you.

'I walkt the other day . . .'

Another meditative poem, in which the poet considers the fields wherein he walks. He decides to dig to find out where the flower was that he had seen before the onset of winter; eventually he finds it living beneath the ground, green and unseen. He learns that the flower will come forth again; he covers him up and weeps, pondering on the fact that the flower beneath is trodden on by everybody. But the poet then invokes God that, through experiences such as these, he may discover the true way to God. The last verse is full of intense personal grief, so that the symbolic edge of the poem and its strongly individual application become apparent. The flower is in its grave but will rise again; the soul will rise beyond the dead body. There is a process of regeneration. In the simplest of God's works is revealed the mystery of all things: the fact that life and death, living and faith, are part of a divine unity.

This is a most moving poem, with the final verses addressed to God taking on a tellingly poignant tone – the poet, like the buried flower, is revealed. There are nine regular 7-line verses in the poem, all having a regular rhyme scheme and a fine ebb-and-flow pattern.

gallant Brave, bold (standing up to the winds and rain).
cold friends i.e. those who do not really care for us.
warm Recluse i.e. snug and alone (but having preserved, if you like, his individual soul!).
strow Throw down, ask.
repair/Such losses i.e. recover from his sufferings.
Come forth i.e. the rebirth of the soul. The whole of this sequence about the flower is symbolic, as we have seen above.
the Clothes i.e. the warm earth (to keep him secure).
frailty Sinfulness.
peace . . . Rock Beautiful words to symbolize, perhaps, rebirth after death.
clod Peasant.
inflame . . . Incubation God bringing out man, creating him.
this frame The world.
Masques i.e. concealments (as in the flower) which hide the mystery of things.
hid ascents Hidden ways of getting to heaven.
Care . . . Light, Joy, Leisure . . . Comforts Note the personification of abstractions in order to bring him the personal quality of the appeal.
his life again . . . I mourn These last three lines are obviously devoted to his dead brother William.

Man

A contemplative poem in which Vaughan considers the permanence of nature as compared with the lack of 'staidness' in man himself. The first verse is given over to an appraisal of nature from birds to bees to the sun; the second verse while glancing at the restless state of man, further emphasizes the harmony of nature and God. The third verse is more specific, with man apparently not knowing his real home, for he moves hither and thither without motive or guidance. The fourth asserts that man has less wit than the stones have, and that he is really a permanent shuttle in motion, without hope of rest. The poem is in four regular 7-line verses.

stedfastness and state The certainty and condition – note the sonorous alliteration in keeping with the content of the poem.

mean Small, of little account (except in the eyes of God).

Intercourse of times The movement and changes in times. Birds are both clock and calendar.

staidness Steadiness, permanence; as the things of nature have stability, so should man.

divine appointments i.e. nature keeps to her appointed role – all things have a particular function ordained by God.

Solomon **was never drest so fine** The reference is to Matthew vi,29: 'even Solomon in all his glory was not arrayed like one of these.'

toyes, or Care i.e. passing amusement or worry.

forgot how to go there i.e. has forgotten his faith and where to find God.

stones . . . point An indication that lodestones are meant because of their magnetic power.

order'd . . . ordain'd Note the fine balance of this.

The Morning-watch

This poem has certain affinities of form and content with Herbert's 'Prayer'. It is an ecstatic ode (though not called that) in praise of all creation: 'The great *Chime*/And *Symphony* of nature.' The movement of the longer lines takes the form of an invocation, that of the shorter a lyrical expression of joy. The whole poem has an exclamatory tone. The final section deals with the ascent of the soul as the ideal, though bed and grave are made synonymous, containing the body which is the servant of God and abides in him.

shoots of glory The growth image typical of this poem, but showing the dual spiritual/natural content that runs through it.

shrouds The first of the death or funeral images.

Blouds i.e. blood creating spirits.

all is hurl'd Note the power of the image, the effect of God being everywhere through the musical images which are to follow this. The musical effect is in fact an orchestration of the harmony of all natural things created by God.

climbe . . . lye down Note the paradox, sleep or rest inducing the ascent of the soul to heaven or to God.

That Curtain'd grave Again note the sonorous and serious movement of this couplet, which rounds off the verse and the ecstasy, and indicates a meditative acceptance.

The Night (John iii,2)

Nine verses of six lines each, with alternate lines rhyming in the quatrain, each verse climaxed by a rhyming couplet. The contemplation of the night, with Nicodemus as the mainspring of the title, for it was in the night that God was revealed to him. But after the detailed biblical associations comes (as so often with Vaughan) the personal involvement with a direct invocation to Night itself, in much the same way as the Elizabethan poets invoked sleep. This is developed throughout the sixth verse with a lyrical poise and fluency, with the conceits elaborated as the verses are unravelled. The poet concludes that he errs more in the daylight than at night, and he longs finally for the night – God – to take him so that he may live 'invisible and dim'.

Virgin-shrine The night as purity and altar of worship.
Nicodemus The Pharisee who supported Jesus against the other Pharisees.
the Sun Christ (a common pun).
dead and silent hour Superb use of paradox, since Nicodemus can speak with Christ at such a time.
No mercy-seat of gold i.e. no old way of dispensing justice (as Jehovah in the Old Testament).
worlds defeat i.e. because it has to stop (the world of men, that is).
cares check and curb i.e. night is an end to worry through sleep.
The day of Spirits A seeming paradox – at night spirits come alive: it is their day.
Christs progress ... i.e. when he prays.
Gods silent, searching flight A reference to the Song of Songs.
The souls dumb watch i.e. silent concentration and communion with other spirits.
Tent Night.
tyre Wear away.
myre Mire.

Peace

This is a fine hymn in praise of God, and the musical sounds are sheer delight. It is a remarkable poem in the sense that the economy and lyricism are unforced, there is a fine control of the quatrains, which are run as one long verse with alternate lines rhyming. And there is a rare simplicity of utterance that is precisely consonant with the mood of exaltation and humility.

Sentrie An angel on guard.
files The ranks of angels.
the flowre of peace i.e. of goodness and tranquillity after a good life.
Rose ... fortresse i.e. Paradise ... protection.
ranges i.e. wanderings.
secure i.e. hold you fast.

Quickness

This poem is an account, brief and symbolic, of the false life as distinct from the 'quickness' of things, which is the insight and truth of God. Beneath the superficial lies reality, the spiritual or divine life apprehended by the intellect. Five quatrains with alternate lines rhyming is the pattern.

a foil i.e. not the main thing.
the true come on i.e. the reality be discovered.
Moon-like i.e. moving, changing.
Self-posing i.e. bewildering – posing unresolved questions.
discerning Seeing into the heart of things.
No chance, or fit No casual or whimsical thing.
vivifie Bring to life.
a toylesom Mole i.e. man.
A quickness The real power and force of life.

Regeneration

This is a complex poem by any standards, and the form contributes to the complexity of the individual experience. There are ten verses of eight lines each. The walk is the beginning of a pilgrimage towards God with the earth the outward show or manifestation of it. The poet weighs the value of his own life, undergoes a mystical experience in which he beholds a new spring, where everything is transfigured in the complete quiet which surrounds it. The grove is obviously a symbol for seeing into the heart of things, and contains the strange hermetic idea that the sun is capable of making minerals. The fountain is the symbol of Christ himself, so that the regeneration of the title has already begun within the poet. The stones he sees represent the souls of men, with the stone that is 'more heavy than the night' the representation of Hell itself. God's presence is in the grove ('the rushing wind'). The next verse establishes that 'God is everywhere', and the poet asks to die before his death is due because of the perfection he has seen in this mystical experience – which is his regeneration and the regeneration of his faith.

A Ward A child.

bonds Imprisoned in the flesh, and hence in sin.

Primros'd A misleading symbol, perhaps, since it may betoken 'the primrose path to the everlasting bonfire' – Hell – as Shakespeare says in *Hamlet*.

frost . . . my mind These lines are symbolic of sin or guilt.

Rough-cast with Rocks, and snow A fine sense of landscape here.

I found a paire of scales Here is the first of the symbols and in the next few lines we see Vaughan weighing his sins.

Jacobs Bed See Genesis xxviii,10 onwards for an account of this. The spirit of God enters the mind – and heart – of man.

he stept i.e. Jacob.

grove Symbolic of an insight into his own heart – the prospect of regeneration, paradise.

unthrift Generous, not careful.

vitall Imbued with vitality, living.

Eare lay hush i.e. I heard nothing.

Fountain A symbol for Christ.

Cisterne For storing the water of the fountain.

divers stones i.e. the various kinds of human souls, both blessed and damned.

Nal'd to the Center i.e. the damned souls are in Hell.

the Ray Of sunlight generally, but in this scene there is little doubt that God is the sun – and the wind.

Where I please i.e. God is everywhere, and I have the power to regenerate myself by serving him and seeing into the heart of things.

The Retreate

A poem in octosyllabic couplets, perfectly controlled with a light fluency and a moving poignancy at the contemplation of a child-hood and innocence that is past. It is this quality which gives the poem universality, for we are bound to see the personal applica-tion to each of us, even if we are not imbued with a like religious motivation. The child is not far removed from Christ, and in nature would see the immortality of the soul and the per-manence of God. This was before the onset of the various forms and practices of sin. The longing is to go back rather than forwards, to the state of closeness to God before the corruption by life began.

second race i.e. because, according to some beliefs, the soul exists before birth.
my first love Christ.
weaker glories i.e. because only reflections of God (in nature).
everlastingnesse i.e. the immortality of the soul.
shady City of Palme trees The ideal of innocence.
stay i.e. remaining on earth too long.
this dust falls i.e. death, hoping that it marks a return to God and innocence.

The Showre

Three 6-line verses, with a simple theme reflecting on a particular scene. The poet sees the moisture rising from the lake in a mist, and then sees the same moisture returning in the form of rain. This scene appears (through the use of the word 'teares') to be an image of repentance. This is certainly overt in the second verse, while the third hopes for the love of God afterwards. These 6-line verses have the first and last lines rhyming in each, with two couplets rhyming (and of different length) in the middle.

Infectious Ease The term speaks of man as well as the lake.
thy mistake Again the connection with sin is obvious.
Exhalations i.e. breathings out (and sighs from the heart).
a Sun-shine after raine i.e. a blessing after sin.

'Silence, and Stealth of dayes! 'tis now'

Another poem consecrated to the loss of William Vaughan. Alternate lines of varying length rhyme alternately; the mood is one of melancholy, with an exact noting of the passage of time since William's death. The poet goes back in time to the actual death scene. But though he cannot recall or recreate the dead man's physical presence, he knows that his soul has gone to heaven. That is where he will see and recognize his brother. Despite the mood, the verse is unforced and almost lyrical, with the analogy of the cave drawn from Plato's *Republic* but used effectively to convey the separation.

stealth i.e. gradual passing.

Twelve hundred houres This counting of the hours since William's death emphasizes the poet's love for his brother and keen sorrow at his loss.

Clouds Sadness.

light . . . lamp Favourite Vaughan images to indicate the light of God and the soul as distinct from the darkness of sin.

defeat/Thy light, and pow'r i.e. when you died.

snuff i.e. the putting out of (a light – a life) just as we snuff out a candle.

the spirit The soul.

Pearle i.e. one source of revelation – presumably the word of God as revealed in the Bible.

The Starre

As one would expect from the title, the invocation is to the star itself, each verse having two rhyming couplets, the first posing the question: what below moves the star? Since all things come from God and therefore have something inherent in their function, the poet will see what he can learn from the star. First he considers the influence of the stars, then their fires, which epitomize desire that will not be quenched; he compares them to magnets because of their influence on the earth. They symbolize celestial thoughts and meanings and act as a kind of mirror-image of the divinity.

stream i.e. with light.

gate Gait, manner of moving.

commerce . . . imbarrs i.e. your contact (does not) inhibit.

subsist . . . Commissions i.e. exist according to the will of God.

the Subject so respected i.e. the star is complete in itself and is respected because of what it represents.

writh'd Made to twist away.

a Commerce states i.e. embodies or establishes a form of communication.

This is the Heart he craves i.e. he wants the worship of men and all created things, for the symbolize his goodness and power, all things are interrelated and exist through God.

'They are all gone into the world of light!'

A wonderful mastery of the quatrain form, with alternate lines rhyming in a balanced, fluent, compelling and poignant poem.

The dead have gone while the poet remains, but they have gone to the world of light; though somehow he is connected with the departed. His vision sees them 'in an Air of glory', and although the contrast with his own state is stressed, he sees them – the departed – as symbolic of the heights to which he may aspire. He then ponders, but lyrically, on the lure of death and the unknown. Angels and Stars draw him, the second by analogy. Finally the poet calls upon God to exert his influence here in this life, or else take him in death.

doth clear Thus giving himself some hope.
remove Departure.
my cold love i.e. because it had not kept within the warmth of God.
Jewel of the Just i.e. because they will enter heaven on the Day of Judgement.
dust i.e. what the body becomes, and whence it came.
outlook that mark See beyond that measure.
strange thoughts Enigmatic, mysterious visions or ideas.
hand that lockt her up i.e. the hand of God. The body is confined to the grave but the soul, so to speak, shines on.
Resume Take on again.
thrall Servitude.
perspective Spy-glass.
unto that hill i.e. death.

The Water-fall

This is another meditative poem symbolizing death and regeneration. There are two verses, the first capturing by its shape and rhythm the movement of the waterfall; the second is an unwinding in couplets of the personal associations and mystical responses to the waterfall, with the idea of the sacredness of baptism very much present.

loose Retinue i.e. other streams, water.
deep and rocky grave i.e. one must pass through this to the longer regeneration – hence this is a symbol.
a sea of light Note the power of the water, here God himself.
That what God takes i.e. since vapour rises to heaven and returns as rain, why should not man rise to heaven?
sacred wash and cleanser i.e. baptism and purification.
Fountains of life . . . Lamb Revelation vii,17.
restagnates all i.e. makes stagnant.
Thou art the Channel i.e. regeneration. These two lines strike a similar note to that sounded by Marvell in 'The Garden'.

The World

This is one of Vaughan's most celebrated poems, with its account of the world as it is, in its various forms and persons. The poem is in the form of a vision, and has a strong allegorical and symbolic significance. The opening is particularly impressive, with its strong personal note, which is to give way to a biting criticism; satirical and ironic appraisals of the lover, the statesman, the miser, the epicure etc. The central symbol is the ring, which is the light of God and hence heaven. The ending is epigrammatic; the bridegroom's ring is for the bride, presumably Christ, but there would appear to be an ascending elect who are capable of joining him.

a great *Ring* i.e. the Universe, and all the manifestations of God.
Lover . . . Complain Cynical at the expense of the poetic lover.
flights Conceits, poetic strains.
sour delights Pleasures that have little to commend them.
his dear Treasure . . . i.e. everything he had valued in life is scattered about him; he has come to the contemplation of the beauty of one of God's created things – a flower.
darksome Melancholy.
weights Responsibilities.
crying witnesses i.e. pestering him, speaking against him.
Yet dig'd the Mole i.e. he had to conceal what he was doing: the comparison with the mole indicates that he is sinful; his doings cannot be tolerated inthe open light of day.
Drank them as free i.e. accepted all things, particularly evil things, without comment and without opposing them.
hug'd . . . pelf Hugged his ill-gotten gains to himself.
in sense The pleasures of the senses.
Excesse Self-indulgence.
triviall wares Inslave They are enslaved by trivial possessions
weep . . . sing Those who were repenting.
tread the Sun Be in heaven, in the highest sphere.
Bride-groome . . . bride i.e. Christ . . . man.

Revision questions on Henry Vaughan

1 Write an essay indicating Vaughan's main religious beliefs.

2 Write an appreciation of Vaughan's use of image and symbol.

3 Write an appreciation of Vaughan as a lyric poet.

4 In what ways is Vaughan primarily a poet of meditation?

5 Write on Vaughan's use of nature in any three poems.

6 What do you find mystical and allegorical in Vaughan's verse?

General questions

1 Write an essay on the microcosmic emphasis in the poetry of John Donne or any other metaphysical poet.

2 Examine the treatment of religion in any one of the poets you have studied.

3 'There is an obsession with death in seventeenth-century verse.' How far would you agree with this comment in relation to any one or two metaphysical poets?

4 Write an essay on metaphysical wit in any two of the poets you have studied.

5 Examine the use of scientific or mathematical or geographical imagery in the work of any one poet you have studied here.

6 By a close study of one or two longer poems, analyse the structure of the poems under consideration and say what this structure contributes to our appreciation.

7 Compare and contrast any two poems of a lyrical nature by two different poets.

8 Write an essay examining either smoothness or roughness in metaphysical poetry, referring to two poets in your answer.

9 Examine the use of the couplet or the quatrain in any two or three poems by the same writer.

10 Write an essay on 'the absurd' in any one or two poets you have studied.

11 Write an essay on the nature of metaphysical love poetry in *either* one or two poets.

13 Examine the use either of song or the elegy in any one or two poets you have studied here.

14 Write an appreciation of any single dialogue poem here.

15 'Elaborate exercises.' Is this, in your view, a fair definition of metaphysical poetry?

Brodie's Notes

Edward Albee	Who's Afraid of Virginia Woolf?
Jane Austen	Emma
Jane Austen	Mansfield Park
Jane Austen	Pride and Prejudice
Samuel Beckett	Waiting for Godot
William Blake	Songs of Innocence and Experience
Robert Bolt	A Man for All Seasons
Charlotte Brontë	Jane Eyre
Emily Brontë	Wuthering Heights
Geoffrey Chaucer	The Franklin's Tale
Geoffrey Chaucer	The Knight's Tale
Geoffrey Chaucer	The Miller's Tale
Geoffrey Chaucer	The Nun's Priest's Tale
Geoffrey Chaucer	The Pardoner's Prologue and Tale
Geoffrey Chaucer	Prologue to the Canterbury Tales
Geoffrey Chaucer	The Wife of Bath's Tale
Wilkie Collins	The Woman in White
William Congreve	The Way of the World
Joseph Conrad	Heart of Darkness
Charles Dickens	Great Expectations
Charles Dickens	Hard Times
Charles Dickens	Oliver Twist
Charles Dickens	A Tale of Two Cities
Gerald Durrell	My Family and Other Animals
George Eliot	The Mill on the Floss
George Eliot	Silas Marner
T. S. Eliot	Selected Poems
Henry Fielding	Tom Jones
F. Scott Fitzgerald	The Great Gatsby and Tender is the Night
E. M. Forster	Howard's End
E. M. Forster	A Passage to India
John Fowles	The French Lieutenant's Woman
Anne Frank	The Diary of Anne Frank
Mrs Gaskell	North and South
William Golding	Lord of the Flies
Graham Greene	Brighton Rock
Graham Greene	The Power and the Glory
Graham Handley (ed)	The Metaphysical Poets: John Donne to Henry Vaughan
Thomas Hardy	Far From the Madding Crowd
Thomas Hardy	The Mayor of Casterbridge
Thomas Hardy	The Return of the Native
Thomas Hardy	Tess of the d'Urbervilles
L. P. Hartley	The Go-Between
Aldous Huxley	Brave New World
Ben Jonson	Volpone
James Joyce	A Portrait of the Artist as a Young Man
John Keats	Selected Poems and Letters of John Keats
Philip Larkin	Selected Poems of Philip Larkin
D. H. Lawrence	The Rainbow
D. H. Lawrence	Sons and Lovers
D. H. Lawrence	Women in Love

List continued overleaf

List continued from previous page

Harper Lee	**To Kill a Mockingbird**
Laurie Lee	**Cider with Rosie**
Christopher Marlowe	**Dr Faustus**
Arthur Miller	**The Crucible**
Arthur Miller	**Death of a Salesman**
John Milton	**Paradise Lost, Books I and II**
Robert C. O'Brien	**Z for Zachariah**
Sean O'Casey	**Juno and the Paycock**
George Orwell	**Animal Farm**
George Orwell	**1984**
J. B. Priestley	**An Inspector Calls**
J. D. Salinger	**The Catcher in the Rye**
William Shakespeare	**Antony and Cleopatra**
William Shakespeare	**As You Like It**
William Shakespeare	**Hamlet**
William Shakespeare	**Henry IV Part I**
William Shakespeare	**Henry IV Part II**
William Shakespeare	**Julius Caesar**
William Shakespeare	**King Lear**
William Shakespeare	**Macbeth**
William Shakespeare	**Measure for Measure**
William Shakespeare	**The Merchant of Venice**
William Shakespeare	**A Midsummer Night's Dream**
William Shakespeare	**Much Ado about Nothing**
William Shakespeare	**Othello**
William Shakespeare	**Richard II**
William Shakespeare	**Richard III**
William Shakespeare	**Romeo and Juliet**
William Shakespeare	**The Tempest**
William Shakespeare	**Twelfth Night**
George Bernard Shaw	**Arms and the Man**
George Bernard Shaw	**Pygmalion**
Alan Sillitoe	**Selected Fiction**
John Steinbeck	**Of Mice and Men and The Pearl**
Jonathan Swift	**Gulliver's Travels**
J. M. Synge	**The Playboy of the Western World**
Dylan Thomas	**Under Milk Wood**
Alice Walker	**The Color Purple**
Virginia Woolf	**To the Lighthouse**
W. B. Yeats	**Selected Poetry**

ENGLISH COURSEWORK BOOKS

Terri Apter	**Women and Society**
Kevin Dowling	**Drama and Poetry**
Philip Gooden	**Conflict**
Philip Gooden	**Science Fiction**
Margaret K. Gray	**Modern Drama**
Graham Handley	**Modern Poetry**
Graham Handley	**Prose**
Graham Handley	**Childhood and Adolescence**
R. J. Sims	**The Short Story**